THAMES VALLEY

WALKS FOR MOTORISTS

Tom Lawrence

30 circular walks with sketch maps

GW00722347

FREDERICK WARNE

Published by
Frederick Warne (Publishers) Ltd
40 Bedford Square
London WC1B 3HE

The photograph on the front cover shows the river Thames at Clifton Hampden (Walk 19) and was taken by Derek Pratt.

Publishers' Note

While every care has been taken in the compilation of this book, the publishers cannot accept responsibility for any inaccuracies. But things may have changed since the book was published: paths are sometimes diverted, a concrete bridge may replace a wooden one, stiles disappear. Please let the publishers know if you discover anything like this on your way.

The length of each walk in this book is given in miles and kilometres, but within the text Imperial measurements are quoted. It is useful to bear the following approximations in mind: 5 miles = 8 kilometres, ½ mile = 800 metres, 1 metre = 39 inches.

ISBN 0 7232 2823 X

Phototypeset, printed and bound by Galava Printing Company Limited, Nelson, Lancs.

Contents

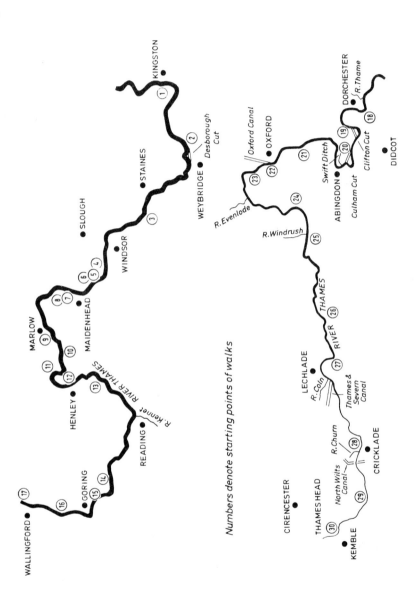

Numbers denote starting points of walks

Introduction

Each walk in this book has been planned to include a section of the Thames towpath, or riverside path, in an upstream direction. Although each circular walk is complete in itself, the idea is that if you undertake all thirty in sequence you will gain a sense of exploring the whole length of the Thames Valley from Kingston Bridge on the outskirts of London to the river's source at Thames Head in a Gloucestershire meadow.

You will see all aspects of the river's constantly changing character, from suburbia, subtly merging into a dramatic central section, and eventually giving way to the peacefulness of the remote upper reaches. Between Godstow and Lechlade no village, let alone a town, lies on the river's bank. In some places the river is hemmed in by towering hills while in others water meadows roll out on either side. A constant feature of every scene, however, is the endless variety of trees, forming patterns against the sky and reflected in the water to leave a lasting memory of beauty.

Yet there is much more than the river in every one of our walks. The Thames Valley countryside of hills, fields and woods which we explore on either side of the river on our circular routes is lovely, too.

The river's route has not always been the one we are about to follow. Once upon a time it flowed into the Wash, but when glacial formations in the last Ice Age pushed it south, the river steadily bored its way through the Chiltern chalk and carved the precipitous Goring Gap. Earlier still, when the North Sea was land, the Thames was a tributary of the Rhine.

We walk with history, too. Since people first settled beside it, the Thames has had strategic significance. It formed the boundary between Saxon Wessex and the Kingdom of Mercia; it was forded by Caesar's invading army and its ancient bridges were fiercely fought over in the Civil War. Bloody massacres, too, have been perpetrated on its banks, not least the appalling 'town and gown' uprising in Oxford in 1355 and the cruel beheading of the defeated garrison of Royalist Wallingford in 1646. As Shelley wrote of this river: 'It runs with the blood and bones of a thousand heroes and villains', adding, however, 'But the scene is most satisfactory, you must agree.' We do.

Because of its unspoilt, typically English (though in no small measure, man-made) scenery, the Thames has long been popular for pleasure tripping. The excursions run by an enterprising Abingdon trader in 1555 to witness the burning at the stake of Latimer and Ridley in Oxford were by no means the first examples of pleasure boating on the river. Today, the constant movement of countless brightly painted pleasure craft adds much to the enchantment of the scene.

Although the river has been navigated by barges since Saxon times its heyday as an artery of trade was, perhaps, in the Middle Ages. Barges then were hauled by gangs of labourers called 'halers' and, over the long stretches that lacked a towpath, poled by the boatmen. With the coming of canals around the end of the eighteenth century the river became an important link in the inland waterways system and navigational improvements were demanded, particularly the provision of pound locks and a continuous towpath. However, for various reasons, including the intransigence of local landowners who refused to have a towpath on their land, it had to be constructed sometimes on one bank and sometimes on the other, requiring the provision of numerous ferries, often with only a short distance between them, to take the towline and horses across. Now that the barges have disappeared the ferries have, of course, gone too.

Not so the locks. The lock cottages beside them, whether modern or a century old, are always pleasing in appearance while the lock-keepers' gardens are invariably beautifully tended and a delight to the eye when we reach them on our rambles.

The Thames Water Authority is responsible for the management of water resources, water supply, pollution control, land drainage, flood alleviation, fisheries and much else, including recreational uses. It welcomes considerate walkers to the towpaths. Not every length of towpath, however, is a right of way, but every length used on our walks, if not a right of way, is a permissive way. Similarly, when we are walking inland from the river on our circular routes, with the exception of one or two footpaths which are permissive ways, all the itineraries in this book utilise public rights of way defined as such on the Ordnance Survey maps. Nevertheless, it must always be remembered that the farmland or woodland through which our paths pass is private property. So bear in mind the Country Code:

The Country Code
Enjoy the countryside and respect its life and work.
Guard against all risk of fire.
Fasten all gates.
Keep your dogs under close control.
Keep to public paths across farmland.
Use gates and stiles to cross fences, hedges and walls.
Leave livestock, crops and machinery alone.
Take your litter home.
Help to keep all water clean.
Protect wildlife, plants and trees.
Take special care on country roads.
Make no unnecessary noise.

The numbers of the Ordnance Survey 1:50,000 sheet, or sheets, which cover the area are given at the head of each walk. The sketch maps provided should be sufficient but a full map unquestionably adds interest to a walk and allows distant features to be identified.

Footwear is the walker's most important equipment. Stout shoes are adequate but boots (worn with two pairs of socks) are better. Although mud is likely to be encountered on any walk anywhere, the Thames Valley seems to have more than its fair share. For this reason there are several walks in this book, mostly in the upper reaches of the river, which I would not recommend in winter or immediately after heavy rain. And always interpret my directions with discretion, for stiles, bridges, signposts and the like may be changed or have disappeared — and almost anything can be eroded by vandals. (One of their favourite tricks is to turn a signpost to face the wrong way.)

That said, none of the rambles should present any real difficulties. The most serious problem likely to be encountered is that of finding a field path ploughed up and planted with crops. Knowing that an inexperienced walker may hesitate to tread through a field of growing corn (despite a desire to keep to the fifth precept in the Country Code), I revised several of my planned itineraries during the course of surveying them when I came up against this sort of obstruction. So, hopefully, it is a difficulty you will not have to face. Yet never forget you have a right — some would say an obligation — to follow a public right of way (but in single file, please) no matter what may be growing on it, for a farmer's failure to reinstate such a footpath after ploughing is quite illegal. Even so, I find it hard to blame you if you feel disposed to follow the line of least resistance rather than the line of a path, and go round the sides of a field. Nevertheless, we are, strictly speaking, trespassing if we stray from the proper right of way.

I said at the beginning that the rambles in this book should give you a sense of exploring the length of the Thames all the way from Kingston to Thames Head. I like to think it is the next best thing to following the long-distance continuous waterside route which is in the process of being established. After 30 years of pressure it is still not quite a reality throughout, for some frustrating gaps remain to be closed. But if, after undertaking the short circular rambles in this volume you feel ready for 156 miles of lineal walking from Putney to the river's source, then a guide entitled *The Thames Walk*, written and illustrated by David Sharp who has been, and is, the chief driving force in this admirable enterprise, can be heartily recommended. *The Thames Walk* is published by the Ramblers' Association at 75p.

4¼ miles (7 km)

OS sheet 176

We have an easy walk to begin with, on much the same level all the way: along the Thames towpath, through the glorious grounds of Hampton Court Palace and back through a delightful Royal park. The walk should not be attempted, however, as dusk approaches or you may find the Palace grounds and the park locked up.

Our starting point is on the Hampton Wick side of Kingston bridge. Just west of the bridge is a roundabout and further west of the roundabout is Kingston Bridge House (an office building), to the side of which is Church Grove. Park in this road. (You may find, unfortunately, that a few other motorists have already had the same idea.)

Walk back to the main road, turn left and cross at the pedestrian crossing to the other side. Go left towards Kingston bridge but just before reaching it drop down on the right to the riverside. The towpath now lies before us and we follow it all the way to Hampton Court. For much of the way the path is shady beneath fine trees. There are wide grassy areas rich with wild flowers and always, on the right, is Hampton Court Park with a glimpse, from time to time, of the Palace in the distance.

Up as far as Teddington lock a couple of miles behind us (which you can't see from here), the level of the river is influenced by the rise and fall of the sea. Here, therefore, we are walking beside the first non-tidal stretch and all the way from here, throughout the 135 miles to the source (measured along the river's twists and turns) the stream is restrained and tamed. Undeniably, we shall find ourselves on later walks beside more attractive reaches than this, yet it is pleasant enough along here and there are some features worth observing.

The eighteenth century tower of Kingston parish church can be seen. In an earlier church on the site, destroyed by the Danes in 1009, seven Saxon kings were crowned, including Ethelred the Unready. The cinema, of which the back is in view, is historic, too. It was one of the very first Odeons, opened in 1933, but is now a bingo hall. The pleasant Queen's Promenade, running towards Surbiton, comes into view, as well as St Raphael's church (1847), looking for all

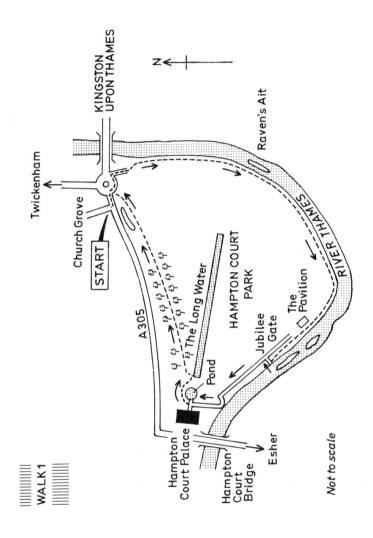

WALK 1

START

Twickenham

Church Grove

KINGSTON
UPON THAMES

A305

The Long Water

Pond

HAMPTON COURT
PARK

Jubilee
Gate

The
Pavilion

Raven's Ait

RIVER THAMES

Hampton
Court Palace

Hampton
Court
Bridge

Esher

N

Not to scale

the world as if it had been miraculously translated from Italy.

There now appears a large island known as Raven's Ait, the site of a conference centre which won a Civic Trust award. We pass the richly wooded Boyle Farm Island then Thames Ditton Island, recognisable by the bungalows there. We pass a private residence on the right called The Pavilion and soon we reach a gate in the wall with a flight of steps. This is the Jubilee Gate, leading into the grounds of Hampton Court Palace.

(If by chance the gate is locked, carry on along the towpath until you can gain access to the Palace. Pass through the Palace—there is no charge—and pick up our walk again one paragraph ahead.)

Through the Jubilee Gate, turn left along a splendid terrace with the river below on the left and a close-mown lawn on the right. At the end of the terrace, where it sweeps round to the left in a great curve, go round with it and then come up the broad path towards the east front of the Palace. This side was designed by Sir Christopher Wren for William III. The earlier, Tudor, palace lies behind, the first part of it having been built by Cardinal Wolsey who offered it to Henry VIII in 1526 in an optimistic, but unavailing, attempt to regain the king's favour. Five of Henry's six wives lived here and the unfortunate Anne Boleyn is said to haunt it still. You may wish to visit the Palace before we go further.

To resume our walk, from the Palace's east-front doorway go towards the Great Fountain in front of it, skirt the fountain to the left and pause for a moment to lean on the iron railings ahead to view the impressive Long Water, a canal constructed by Charles II. Then turn left, cross an iron footbridge and enter, through gates, Hampton Court Park, or 'Home Park', as it is often called. Proceed down the centre of the broad avenue of trees ahead. With luck, you may encounter a herd of fallow deer.

Ignore a gravelled crossing path. The avenue of trees ends and there is an open, green area before the trees begin again. At this point bear slightly left and make your way along the right-hand side of a lake where some seats are conveniently placed for a well-earned rest.

However, we are near the end of our journey, and Kingston Gate has already come into sight. Pass through the gate and cross the road to Church Grove, where you left your car.

2½ miles (4 km)

OS sheet 176

This easy, short walk, on excellent paths throughout, is the only walk in the book to follow water all the way. It would make an enjoyable stroll on a summer's day.

The starting point is the free car park on the minor road that branches off to the left just before the 'temporary' Walton Bridge. Left, that is to say, if you are approaching from the Walton side, but on the right, of course, if you are coming from the Shepperton side.

Having safely parked the car, cross the road and the wide grass verge beside it to reach the towpath at just about the point where, they say, Caesar forded the river with his army. Turn left. Unfortunately the first half mile does not offer anything very much in the way of views since the opposite bank is occupied by a long row of small riverside dwellings. It was different when Caesar saw it in BC54 during his second invasion, for there was then an imposing force of Britons drawn up to oppose him. He wrote an account of the battle, saying that the bank was planted with sharp stakes, and similar stakes were embedded beneath the water. One of the stakes, found in the river in 1777 when the water was running exceptionally low, may be seen in the British Museum.

When you come to the bridge crossing the entrance to the Desborough Channel, go up the steps onto the bridge and cross it. The Desborough Channel, as you will see, looks like a wide canal — which is in fact what it is. At the end of the slope off the bridge we go forward by the riverside, making our way at first along a little road at a University Vandals RFC sign. When this road bends left go ahead along a tree-lined path beside the river and before long you will find a pleasant, open space spreading out to the left. This is the Surrey County Council's Point Meadow.

Soon the tower of the 'new' Shepperton Church comes into view, 'new' because it was built in 1613 to replace an earlier church washed away by the river. We cannot visit it, unfortunately, because it is on the other side of the river.

The Thames and its towpath meander round the meadow in a great left-hand curve known as the Halliford Bend. When the path leaves the waterside to bear left and climb up to an iron gate we have to

11

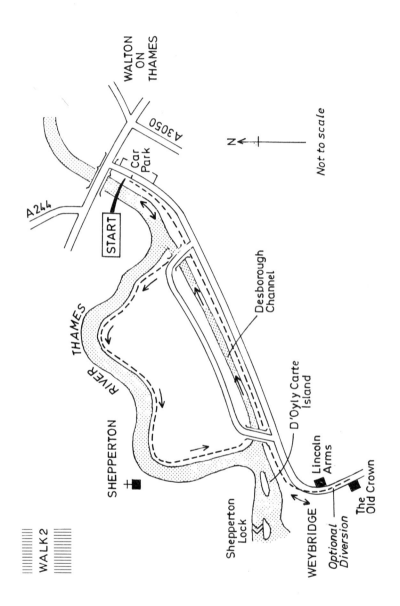

WALK 2

WALTON ON THAMES

A3050

A244

Car Park

START

RIVER THAMES

SHEPPERTON

Desborough Channel

D'Oyly Carte Island

Lincoln Arms

Shepperton Lock

WEYBRIDGE

Optional Diversion

The Old Crown

N

Not to scale

12

follow the path, for here is the bridge over the Desborough Channel where it rejoins the river. On the far side, turn right down a steep flight of steps to the towpath.

Now, if you wish to make an optional diversion into Weybridge (the southernmost point of the Thames), carry on along the towpath for a few hundred yards. On the way you will pass D'Oyly Carte Island, on which was the summer residence of Richard D'Oyly Carte, the impresario of the Gilbert and Sullivan operas at the Savoy Theatre from 1877 onwards. Just beyond the inland the river widens at Shepperton Lock and weir and you are obliged to bear left onto a road beside the Wey Navigation. This was once a busy spot, where traffic from several island waterways converged upon the Thames. The river Wey was 'canalised' in the mid-seventeenth century, allowing a flourishing water-borne trade to Guildford, and later the navigation was extended to Godalming. The Basingstoke Canal, which joined the Wey near Byfleet, was opened in 1796 and the Wey Arun Junction Canal, running from Shalford on the Wey south of Guildford, in 1816. Thus was the Thames linked from here to the South Coast.

What you probably had in mind when you diverted to Weybridge now materialises: the Lincoln Arms is already visible, while the Old Crown, an attractive weather-boarded inn, lies just round the corner.

The walk proper, however, continues along the towpath of the Desborough Channel, which was built during the early 1930s and opened by Lord Desborough (Chairman of the Thames Conservancy from 1904 to 1937) in 1935. Although the Channel is fairly straight it is by no means unattractive. The fine trees on the opposite bank have grown, presumably, since the channel was dug. Our side is pleasant enough, too, apart from the road which runs parallel to the towpath. We can hardly see it since we are below its level but unfortunately we can hear the traffic upon it.

We come to the end of the Desborough Channel, pass under the bridge and find ourselves on the towpath on which we began the walk. Ahead is Walton Bridge. There has been more than one bridge here since the first was completed in 1750. A wooden structure, it had become ruinous by 1780, although not before Canaletto had painted it. It was replaced by a stone and brick bridge which Turner painted, but in 1859 a great storm swept part of it away and an iron bridge was built in its place. By 1954 it had become unsafe and the 'temporary' one, which is still in use, was built beside it. By the time you have absorbed all this you will have come abreast of the car park where you left your car.

Walk 3

Runnymede

3½ miles (5.5 km)

OS sheet 176

I cannot decide whether this walk qualifies for a place in the book's Top Ten or not. There are walks in more picturesque countryside or which include much longer and more attractive reaches of the Thames and there are walks more peaceful and quiet, for a substantial part of this one is within sight and sound of busy roads. Yet Runnymede clearly demands a place not only as one of the most notable sites beside the Thames but as one of the most famous in all England. In fact, this walk is something of an experience, for we tread on a meadow steeped in history, on a patch of soil that is, literally, American and — on a hill top — on holy ground.

In distance, this walk is not long but it is moderately strenuous in that there is a hill to be climbed (although the view from the top is worth it). The starting point is Egham, a small town just west of Staines and by-passed by the A30. There are two or three free car parks, the most convenient from our point of view being in Hummer Road, a residential road running to the left of The Catherine Wheel, almost opposite the church.

Walk down Hummer Road, cross the busy A30 carefully and take the clear asphalt path ahead across part of Runnymede. Cross the A308 and go down narrow Yard Mead, opposite, to the river and turn left along the towpath. When the riverside bungalows soon come to an end keep near the water as the river sweeps round in a curve to the left and then right. The other side of the river is densely wooded while on our side there is a recreational park. As we turn right with the river we catch a glimpse of the white tower of the Commonwealth Air Forces Memorial high up on wooded Cooper's Hill ahead. The river along the next stretch is often hidden from view by trees and bushes that have grown up along the water's edge.

Pass through a grassy area used as a small car park at a National Trust sign and soon you will see, over to your left, a sign pointing to the Magna Carta Memorial and the John F. Kennedy Memorial. Cross the road and go over the field to the Magna Carta Memorial, erected by the American Bar Association to commemorate the granting of Magna Carta, a 'symbol of freedom under law', in these meadows, on 15 June, 1215. The exact spot where the reluctant King

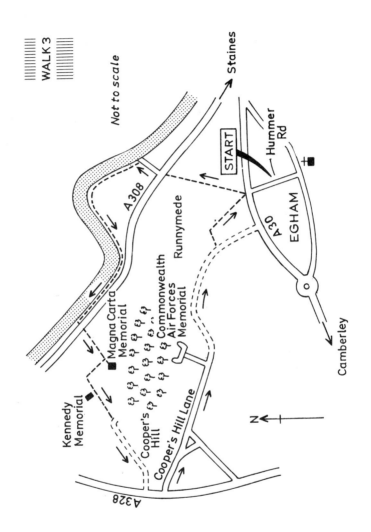

WALK 3

Not to scale

Staines

Hummer Rd

START

EGHAM

A30

A308

Runnymede

Camberley

Magna Carta Memorial

Commonwealth Air Forces Memorial

Cooper's Hill

Kennedy Memorial

Cooper's Hill Lane

N

A328

John put pen to parchment is uncertain.

After visiting the memorial, turn left outside the gate and make your way along the meadow, a hedge on your left, to the entrance to the John F. Kennedy Memorial and follow the winding path and steps up Cooper's Hill towards it. Simple, yet impressive, it stands on an 'acre of English ground ... given to the United States of America by the people of Britain' in memory of a president who died by an assassin's hand.

Continue on the path climbing up the hill behind and to the left of the memorial (but *not* the little path going off left at a right angle to it). The path becomes a drive and goes ahead, with the glorious park-like grounds of the Shoreditch College of Brunel University on the left, to the A328. On reaching the road turn left, keeping to a rough path on the wide grass verge. We very soon leave the road, however, by turning left into Cooper's Hill Lane, signposted 'Air Forces Memorial'.

The memorial should be visited not so much for the superb views, especially from the tower, of river and meadow, but for a deeply moving experience. The Commonwealth Air Forces Memorial, designed by Sir Edward Maufe (architect of Guildford Cathedral) and opened by The Queen in 1953 is a beautiful place, impeccably kept and inexpressibly sad. Carved on its cloister walls are 20,455 names of those who have no known graves. In her address, Her Majesty quoted the curiously prophetic lines of the poet Pope, referring to the hill on which we stand:

> *On Cooper's Hill eternal wreaths shall grow*
> *While lasts the mountain, or while Thames shall flow.*

On leaving the memorial, turn left. The road soon bends left, becoming a rough lane or track, and bends to the right, descending quite steeply the wonderfully wooded hillside. Eventually we come to a stile on the left—be careful not to miss it because of bushes— just past a National Trust sign. Cross the stile and go down the sloping field towards a stile in the form of concrete blocks to help one over a fence.

Now the point to make for is the top of Hummer Road, midway along the row of houses to be seen half-right ahead. Officially, the path goes straight towards it, across the meadow. But, probably because the meadow can be marshy, paths seem to have been trodden out which more or less skirt round the right-hand edge of it and I doubt if anyone will mind if you go that way. I wish you could walk backwards here, for the view behind, unlike the view in front, is splendid.

Before long you converge on the beginning of the clear asphalt path on which we started our walk over Runnymede. On the other side of the A30 is Hummer Road and the car park.

4 miles (6.5 km)

OS sheet 175

This is an easy, enjoyable walk. The stretch beside the Thames is very attractive, there are some interesting things to see, it is all on the same level and no difficulties are likely to be encountered. A few steps at the beginning and end of the walk duplicate Walk 5.

The starting point is near the hamlet of Boveney, which is reached along a minor road running south from the B3026 as it crosses Dorney Common on its way from Eton to Taplow (near which it intersects the A4). The common seems like something from an earlier age. The road is unfenced and herds of cows roam all over the place. By Boveney Court the road bends sharply left (Lock Path) and it should be possible to park on a patch of fairly rough grass a little further on to the right and just short of a much larger piece of grass which, as numerous notices warn us, is reserved as a private parking space for an angling club.

We start our walk by continuing along Lock Path, ignoring a path bearing right towards the chapel of St Mary Magdalene, and pass through a gate leading to an avenue of fine chestnut trees. When the trees end and the lane bends right to Boveney Lock we go ahead on a rough bridleway (not signposted) at the right-hand edge of a field. This bridleway eventually leads right through a gap in the hedge and comes to the riverside at a small concrete bridge over a stream where it joins the Thames.

Cross the bridge and immediately turn half-left along a bridleway through the middle of a field—in other words, keep to an angle of rather more than 45 degrees to the towpath. When a crossing track is met, turn right, heading slightly to the left of Windsor Castle ahead and towards the five elegant arches beneath the busy Windsor by-pass road, from which the traffic noise will, alas, grow louder as you approach. The great grey edifice of the castle, enshrining as it does a thousand years of our history, is a grand sight for us to contemplate as we make our way across the field.

Yet actually, much of the Castle is not all that old, for tremendous alterations and additions were carried out by Charles II, George III, George IV (who spent well over £1 million, a lot of money in those days) and Queen Victoria. In fact, much of the exterior, as well as the

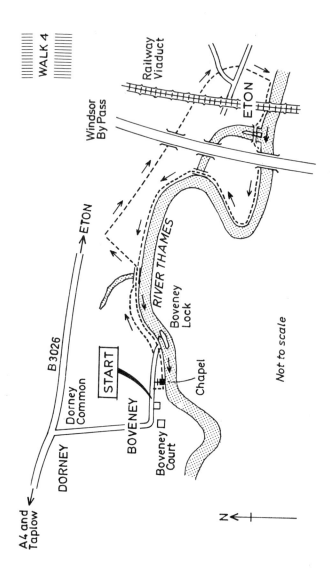

WALK 4

Railway Viaduct

Windsor By Pass

ETON

→ ETON

B 3026

Dorney Common

START

BOVENEY

DORNEY

Boveney Court

Chapel

Boveney Lock

RIVER THAMES

ETON

A4 and Taplow

Not to scale

N ←

upper part of Henry II's great Round Tower, is nineteenth century, the work of an architect named Wyatville, who was responsible for demolishing many of the older parts of the Castle. Nothing of the original Norman remains. No wonder the official guide calls it a 'fairy tale creation.'

Another interesting feature as you approach the arches beneath the by-pass road is the contrast between their modern style and that of the arches of the nineteenth century railway viaduct to be seen ahead.

Pass beneath the by-pass road and our path now continues towards Eton College Chapel. On the other side of the impressive railway viaduct, which seems more suited to Queen Victoria's royal train than the two-car diesel sets that cross it today, our way lies half-right across a playing field (the path actually starts a few feet to the left) to a gap in the hedge. Through this, we go left along a good path at the left-hand edge of another playing field. (I don't think these Eton playing fields are those on which the battle of Waterloo was won.)

Go over a narrow, but busy, road to a small gate opposite and cross another field, now heading at first just to the right of the castle. On reaching a small car park immediately turn right and cross a road to a stile and make your way, leftish, over the field to the Thames and turn right along the towpath.

We pass beneath a railway bridge, over two iron footbridges and under the by-pass road and the best part of our walk now begins. This attractive reach of the river is wide and wooded. As it sweeps round in a sharp right-hand bend, notice an iron post scored by the tow-ropes of horse-drawn barges of many years ago.

A wooden footbridge takes us over a backwater of the river; the two iron footbridges we crossed earlier were at the other end of it. The next bridge we come to, some way further on, is the little concrete footbridge we crossed when our route touched the river near the beginning of our walk. We cross it again and carry on along the towpath. The character of it changes now, with bushes on either side, until we come to Boveney Lock, a particularly charming spot, I'm told, at lilac time.

Go past the lock, along the towpath, to the tiny riverside chapel of St Mary Magdalene, parts of which are twelfth century. Turn right onto the path past the chapel and soon come to the parking place where, a little to the left, you left your car.

19

Walk 5   Dorney

5½ or 5 miles (9 or 8 km)

OS sheet 175
This walk may be combined with Walk 6

There is a nice long stretch of the river to be followed on this walk, the paths throughout are good and no difficulties are likely to be encountered.

Dorney, our starting point, is an attractive village on the B3026, the road from Eton to just north of Taplow. It intersects the A4 at a roundabout. Near the top end of the village a minor road, signposted 'Dorney Reach', turns off. Take this road and park discreetly, perhaps on a patch of rough ground just past St James's Church, although you may have difficulty in seeing the church as it is grouped with Dorney Court and lies partly hidden by buildings. It is just before the road does a sharp right-hand bend. This is where we start walking.

Begin by turning round upon yourself and going back along the road towards Dorney village. You may care to visit the church first, however, for you will find it extremely interesting. Of flint construction with a sixteenth century brick tower, it has an air, unlike the majority of churches, of having stayed unchanged for many years and even seems to have been spared Victorian restoration. It is lit by seventeenth century candelabra, and worth seeing are the high-sided family pew, 400 years old, and a tremendous monument to a sixteenth century knight, his wife and fifteen children. At the west end the seventeenth century gallery is still intact.

Before reaching the end of the road there is another attraction. We pass the entry to Dorney Court, said to be one of the finest manor houses in Britain, and open on certain days during the summer. You may wish to visit it if you have picked one of the right days. A famous gardener employed here grew the first pineapple in England, hence, no doubt, The Pineapple pub in the village.

At the T-junction turn right, cross the road and make your way through Dorney village, passing the Palmers Arms on the left and then, on the right, what must surely be one of the few Tudor petrol filling stations and motor repair workshops anywhere. But Dorney, as you will have observed, is rich in lovely old Tudor buildings.

Having crossed a cattle grid we are on Dorney Common. After passing a farm entrance on the right, you will find a path on the

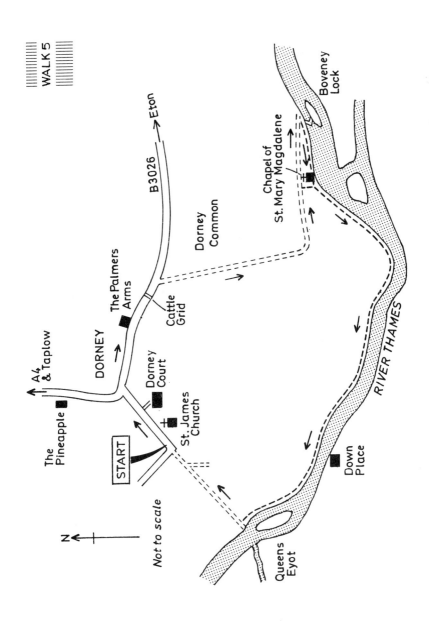

WALK 5

The Pineapple

A4 & Taplow

DORNEY

The Pineapple

The Palmers Arms

B3026 → Eton

START

Dorney Court

St. James Church

Cattle Grid

Dorney Common

Chapel of St. Mary Magdalene

Boveney Lock

RIVER THAMES

Down Place

Queens Eyot

N ←

Not to scale

common running parallel with the road and a few yards from it. This soon curves round to the right and we follow it round, now parallel with a little road signposted 'Boveney'. Even when the path peters out you can still walk on the grass if you wish. Windsor Castle becomes visible in the distance on the left.

At Boveney Court we turn left along Lock Path. At the end of the piece of rough ground which serves as a parking place for the exclusive use of members of MASDA (Maidenhead Angling Society and District Association) there is a footpath sign by the entrance to a path away to the right. If you *must* take this short cut, do so and it will bring you past the chapel of St Mary Magdalene and onto the Thames towpath. Turn right here, and skip the next paragraph. But the short cut will not shorten the walk by very much and you will miss an attractive part of it.

The rest of us go forward over a cattle grid by a (presently vandalised) footpath sign, along a lovely avenue of chestnut trees and come to Boveney Lock. Here we turn right along the towpath after pausing for a while to enjoy the sight of a variety of craft going up and down through this picturesque lock. Soon after leaving the lock we reach the isolated chapel of St Mary Magdalene.

The chapel was not always lonely for this was a busy spot in former times, a nearby wharf being in constant use for the shipping of timber from Windsor Forest. Parts of the chapel are twelfth and thirteenth century and services are held occasionally.

Two miles or so of wholly pleasant waterside walking, with wide open country on the right, lie ahead on a path which, although sometimes narrow, is always good. On the other side of the water the scenery is not so attractive all the way, including a caravan site and the like. Even so, there are exceptions. Down Place, which will also come into view, is a quite remarkable edifice often used, I understand, as a film location. You won't be needing my help along here so put the book into your pocket until you come abreast of a large wooded island known as Queen's Eyot, which belongs to Eton College.

Soon after passing the far end of the Eyot you will see a path leading off from the towpath by a Thames Conservancy sign and opposite the point where a small tributary enters the Thames. Turn right along this path*, which soon becomes a track and you will notice Windsor Castle again, now to your right. When another track joins from the right carry on ahead (at a warning notice saying 'Armed Trespassers will be Prosecuted, by Order') and in a couple of hundred yards or so you will come to the road by the side of which you left your car.

Do visit St James's church if you didn't before setting out.

* If you are combining this walk with Walk 6, carry on along the towpath and pick up the itinerary from the fourth paragraph of Walk 6.

Walk 6 Bray

3½ miles (5.5 km)

OS sheet 175
This walk may be combined with Walk 5

The star attraction of this easy walk is picturesque Bray Lock, one of the loveliest on the Thames and one which, not surprisingly, has won the Lock Garden Competition many times.

The starting point is near Dorney Church. Dorney, an attractive village rich in Tudor buildings, lies on the B3026, the road that runs from Eton to join the B476 near Taplow and which intersects the A4 at a roundabout. In Dorney village turn into the minor road signposted 'Dorney Reach' and park discreetly, perhaps on the patch of rough ground near where the road bends very sharply, close to St James's Church. (This is the same starting point as for the previous walk.)

By the sharp bend, go along Barge Lane, a stony lane at a 'Public Footpath and Bridleway' sign. At the fork, keep right. A pleasant short walk to the riverside lies ahead. On reaching the towpath, turn right.

Before long we pass Monkey Island. In a fishing lodge (now demolished) on the island, an eighteenth century artist painted — a typical eighteenth century conceit — scenes with monkeys dressed like fashionable ladies and gentlemen of the time engaged in fishing and boating. The paintings are still to be seen in the present Monkey Island Hotel.

The way here is garden-like; the grass is mown and there are houses on the right calculated to test to the uttermost one's adherence to the Tenth Commandment. Then, suddenly, all is changed and we find ourselves on a narrow path through bushes so thick that the river, although only a few feet away, can hardly be seen.

Soon we pass beneath the bridge carrying the M4 motorway over the river. Although our walk carries on along the towpath ahead, you may wish to peel off for a while to visit Bray or the Monkey Island Hotel. Steps up to the bridge and pedestrian ways across it have thoughtfully been provided for just such an eventuality. If the hotel is your aim, it is preferable to take the first steps you come to; if sightseeing or shopping, make the crossing on the upstream side. You will remember, of course, that Bray Church is where, if you had come 400 years earlier, you might have met the famous Vicar who was twice

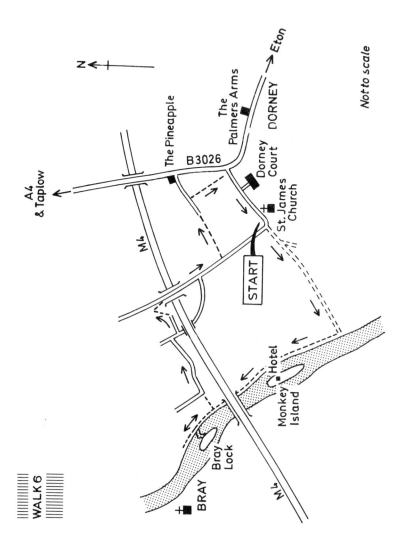

WALK 6

N

A4 & Taplow

The Pineapple

B3026

M4

The Palmers Arms

DORNEY → Eton

Dorney Court

St. James Church

START

Hotel

Monkey Island

M4

Bray Lock

BRAY

Not to scale

24

a Roman Catholic and twice an Anglican. He was Simon Aleyn, appointed in the time of Henry VIII, who kept his living during the reigns of the next three sovereigns by changing his views to correspond with theirs.

And then we come to Bray Lock. Before reaching the lock, however, notice a wide gravel path leading away from the waterside. After visiting the lock we shall return and take this path. But don't neglect to visit the lock and perhaps rest there for a while to watch the boats going through. Walk a little way past the lock, too, for its most enchanting display of lawns and flower beds in an explosion of colour lies on the upstream side.

When you can tear yourself away, come back to the path we noticed before we reached the lock and turn along it. It comes out into a lane at a corner where we turn right and carry on ahead. At a T-junction of lanes and a house called Rookwood, turn right. The lane is rudely cut off not far ahead by the M4 so that it is necessary for us to turn left just short of the motorway, along a private road at a 'No Cycling' sign. At the end of this road we come to a zig-zag path which brings us up onto the bridge over the busy road. Cross the bridge and carry on along the road ahead.

Before long you will see a stile on the left by a footpath sign. This is our way. The path goes across a field to a stile, on the other side of which is a plank bridge over a ditch and another stile. The path then goes up the left-hand side of a field to another stile and then by the side of another field to a stile leading into a cart track.

When a stile appears in the hedge on the right, hesitate. If you carry on up the track for a short distance, you will come to The Pineapple, a 'real ale' pub whose name commemorates the first growing of a pineapple in England at nearby Dorney Court.

Our walk, however, continues across the stile and along the left-hand side of the field, a barbed wire fence on the left, to a stile leading into Court Lane. Turn right in the lane and soon you will reach the corner near which you parked your car. But before getting there you will pass the entrance to Dorney Court and then St James's Church. There are some notes about both these places of interest in the previous walk. Do visit the church before going home, it's fascinating.

Walk 7   Cliveden

5½ miles (9 km)

OS sheet 175
This walk may be combined with Walk 8

An easy and interesting ramble. A bit in the middle is, perhaps, a trifle dull, but on the other hand the earlier section is delightful. There is a visit to Boulter's Lock, which is usually described as the most famous lock on the Thames, while the length of towpath we cover today is along Cliveden Reach, regarded by many as the most beautiful part of the river.

The starting point is the small, free car park on Cookham Moor, the same starting point as for Walk 8. Cookham village lies on the A4094 which runs north from Maidenhead to Bourne End. Cookham is only a couple of miles from Maidenhead and Cookham Moor is reached by turning west onto the B4447 in the village. The car park will be found on the right-hand side, a short distance past the last of the buildings.

We start our walk by turning left out of the car park towards Cookham village, but before reaching the war memorial cross the grass on the right towards a footpath sign. This indicates our way. The path has trees on the left and, on the right, a wall which soon gives place to railings revealing a wide, open view.

The path bends right after a while, with the railings, and comes to a sort of stile. It then continues, with railings still on the right, along the edge of a field and reaches another stile. Beyond this we cross a drive and carry on along the very pleasant path ahead at the right-hand edge of a large field. Soon we find ourselves walking beside an elongated pond called Strand Water and we stay beside this as we leave the field and enter the next.

At the end of this field the path divides, the right fork going across a small footbridge and the left fork — the route we must take — running first between railings and then along the left-hand edge of another field, with iron railings on our left. This struck me as rather an unusual feature in an agricultural environment like this.

Top marks, by the way, to the farmer (or farmers) around here, and our thanks to them for leaving the footpaths undisturbed by plough-ing, unlike some of their brethren elsewhere on our walks.

We come to another stile and beyond it our path bears right to run near the right-hand edge of a field which is National Trust property. The path is only faintly visible on the ground but that does not matter

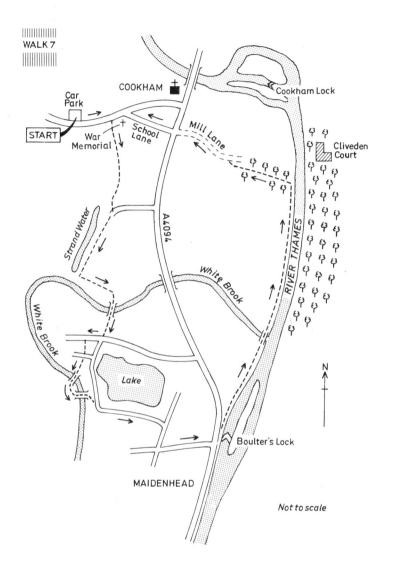

as it leads towards a stile which is to be seen ahead. When we get near it we see, too, that before reaching it there is a narrow footbridge over White Brook to be negotiated.

Safely over the brook and over the stile, the path carries on along the left-hand edge of a field, heading directly towards the spire of a Maidenhead church in the distance. At the end of the field, by a double footpath sign, we come to an iron stile of an unusual pattern I

27

have never seen before but redundant, because one can walk round it. Here turn right along a stony lane.

After a couple of hundred yards the lane bends right but we go left along a signposted path to another of these unusual iron stiles. As you negotiate it you will probably wonder why such an excellent design of stile is not in more general use. Our path then goes slightly more than half-left across the field to another stile we can see in the hedge at the other side of the field and, as we cross the field, a view opens up on the left of a lake and yachts with multi-coloured sails.

Over the stile — a conventional one, this time — we cross a stony lane and over another of the splendid iron stiles. Now we can see the lake and the yachts more closely from our path as it runs through the middle of the field. We cross a footbridge over the same White Brook that we crossed earlier, and immediately turn left beside it. A path coming in from the right merges with ours and soon we cross the brook for the third time by another footbridge. We come then to another of my favourite stiles, beyond which the path meets a rough lane by a double footpath sign and we turn right. Some sand and gravel workings on the left here are not picturesque, but interesting.

At an iron gate, by the entrance to the Summerleaze Pit, we bear right into a residential road (Summerleaze Road) at a corner and turn left. Half a mile of road walking lies ahead of us unfortunately (but unavoidably) till we reach Boulter's Lock. The road bends right and comes to a crossing road (Sheephouse Road) at which we turn right and then to a crossroads at which we turn left (Ray Mill Road East). This soon joins the main road (A4094) on the other side of which is the river Thames, Boulter's Lock and an elegant balustraded bridge linking with an island, on which stand Boulter's Inn and an old mill ('boulter' is an old name for a miller).

I suppose Boulter's Lock is always called the most famous lock on the river because it is so easy to get to, lying as it does beside a main road. On a summer day it is thronged with people, as it was in Edwardian days when it was *the* fashionable boating centre. But I promise you that other walks in this book will take in some lovelier locks than this and ones you will be able to enjoy without such a stifling press of people.

Our walk continues along the road, the river on the right, for a short distance beyond the lock until we leave the road where the towpath diverges from it. The river seems narrow here but this is because we are still walking level with the island, which is quite a big one. When we have passed its tip, however, and the water has widened out, the most glorious views of the Cliveden woods open up; great beech woods that sweep down to the river's edge.

Just beyond the last of the rather grand riverside houses we cross — positively for the last time — the White Brook, where it empties itself into the Thames.

We have some way to go along the towpath before the great house, Cliveden Court, comes into dramatic view high on the hillside. The present building was designed by Sir Charles Barry, the architect of the Houses of Parliament, after a fire of 1849 and was bought by an American, William Waldorf Astor, in 1893. Today house, garden and hanging woods are in the hands of the National Trust.

Eventually we come to a point where, at the site of the old strangely-named My Lady Ferry (the remains of the landing stage are slowly falling into decay) we can go no further beside the water. So here we must turn left to follow a clear path near the edge of woodland. Be a little careful when the main path forks right to join an asphalt drive for our route lies along the path's left fork, ahead, which is slightly overgrown. At the end of the path you will come to a footpath sign and then, on the other side of a drive, to another sign pointing to a 'Public Footpath', a broad path which brings us out into Mill Lane opposite the entrance to a house called The Sol, and we turn left.

This peaceful lane skirts a cricket field and comes out eventually to the main road, the A4094.

Now you can either take the quiet School Lane opposite which by-passes Cookham's main street, or turn right for a couple of hundred yards and then left at the Stanley Spencer Gallery into the High Street if you want to sample the village's fleshpots: the tea rooms and the shops or the pubs, of which it seems to have more than its share.

Cookham would be much nicer if it were not so choked by cars. Holy Trinity Church was a favourite subject of Sir Stanley Spencer, who lived in the village until his death in 1959 and is famous for his mystical paintings. One of his works, *The Last Supper*, hangs in the church. Due to the weight of the roof, the north and east walls of the church are leaning outwards but as they have been doing so for 800 years they will doubtless stand up until after your visit.

Whichever route you take we shall meet near the war memorial. The car park is only a short distance ahead, on the right.

Walk 8   Cookham

4 miles (6.5 km)

OS sheet 175
This walk may be combined with Walk 7

A little gentle climbing has to be done on this walk, but nothing strenuous. This is a varied ramble, on good paths throughout, with many pleasant views to be enjoyed although it is not the riverside section that, on the whole, offers the most attractive scenery.

Our walk starts in the small free car park on Cookham Moor, the same starting point as for Walk 7. Cookham village is on the A4094 which runs north from Maidenhead to Bourne End (Cookham is only a couple of miles from Maidenhead) and Cookham Moor is reached by turning west onto the B4447 in the village. The car park lies on the right-hand side, a short distance past the last of the buildings.

Make your way back to the village, past the war memorial and along the High Street, which contains some lovely old buildings and a plentitude of pubs, and come to the main road. Turn left in the direction signposted to Bourne End and Wooburn. First, however, at the top of the High Street you will notice the Stanley Spencer Gallery, which houses paintings by Sir Stanley Spencer who lived in Cookham until his death in 1959. He is especially noted for his paintings of Christ in a modern English setting, and Cookham churchyard, which we shall pass through in a minute, features in his works.

There is something else of interest to see before we go much further; the Tarry Stone (a meteorite, maybe) on the opposite side of the road 'at which' says a notice, 'sports were held before AD 1507'.

Almost at once, turn left into Church Gate, signposted 'Cookham Church', and enter the churchyard, taking the good path past the west end of the church and thankfully noting that the occupants of the graves are resting in peace and not resurrecting as in Spencer's most famous picture.

Through a kissing gate we come to the Thames where we turn left along the towpath. The first couple of hundred yards are park-like and the boats moored along the water's edge contribute to a pleasant scene. We pass Cookham Reach Sailing Club's premises and then we are in open country. Our way is now along the towpath for nearly two miles, so ignore the footpath running left from the first wooden gate you come to. This stands by an odd little bridge that does no more than allow water from the river to supply a drinking pool for cattle.

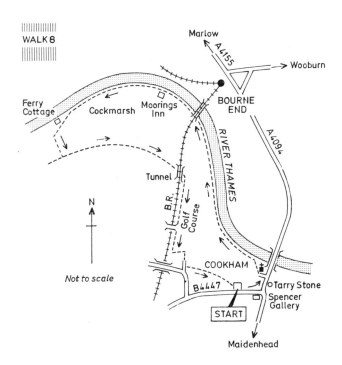

We pass through another wooden gate almost opposite Andrews Boathouses and then find our path shaded by a long line of trees, many of them ancient willows with curiously riven trunks. We pass under a railway bridge and the scene changes again. Boats are moored on either side of the river and, on our side, there is a string of small bungalows and chalets. Now comes the Moorings Inn with its riverside bar inviting a stop, especially as it is the only one, a notice informs us, between here and Henley.

A few more small dwellings are passed and then a gate leads into Cockmarsh, a wide open space owned by the National Trust. Another gate and a little bridge over a dried-up stream take us out of Cockmarsh and by the side of a very large field with trees interposed between our path and the river. You may observe, as you pass it, a now quite useless gate on the right, apparently indicating that the towpath, with the passage of time, has moved itself a few feet inland; the result of bank erosion, perhaps.

Soon we arrive at Ferry Cottage, a pretty white-painted house. The ferry, of course, has long gone so there is no way of reaching the towpath which continues on the other bank. Our towpath walk, therefore, ends here, but happily a path continues, although it bears gradually away from the waterside as it passes to the left of the cottage

31

and behind some chalets. Soon, too, it bends sharply left, running towards a footpath sign beside an elaborate stile of wood, concrete and iron which it is much easier to go round than over.

The path then leads across the field towards a wooded hill ahead. At the end of the field we come to another stile, which this time we are obliged to climb, and go forward a short distance to a clear wide track running from right to left. We turn left upon it, ignoring at least six other small paths going off in all directions. Our route is on the level, at the base of the hill.

Eventually we reach an exceedingly high stile and, after negotiating it, our path lies ahead along a tree-lined way towards a little railway tunnel. Just before it, however, the main path seems to swerve right and then left. Through the tunnel and at a footpath sign, we cross a stile on the right and go up some steep steps to reach — at a footpath sign erected by the East Berks Group of the Ramblers' Association — the Winter Hill Golf Course.

At once a notice cautions us that the path crosses the golf course. Fearlessly, however, we step out right and follow the path. It climbs gently at first until a steep, but short, stretch takes us up to a bridge over the railway. At this point we get our best view of the day — a panorama of the river. It looks much lovelier from here than it did from the towpath, with glorious wooded hills behind.

We do not cross the bridge but carry on ahead at the edge of the golf course — even more bravely now as we pass a notice saying 'Beware Flying Golf Balls'. The path turns left at a corner of the golf course, a yellow distant signal by the railway seeming to point our way. With first a hedge on the right, the path soon bends right, now with wire fencing on the right. We come to a stile and cross it. Two drives lie ahead and we take the left one in a forward direction until, just before reaching a narrow road, we turn left down a signposted path past a house called 'Fiveways'. The path goes to the right of a large wooden field gate you can see ahead; the path is narrow and there is a stout wooden fence on its left. It ends at a stile.

Cross the stile and go half-right beside a willow-lined stream. The path reaches a stile and beyond it a rough concrete bridge spans the stream. The path then leads on through the bushes and comes out in the car park, in which you left your car.

4 miles (6.5 km)

OS sheet 175

A gentle walk with no gradients or difficulties, and there are several interesting things to see.

Marlow lies on the A4155 which runs from Henley-on-Thames to Bourne End. The town can also be conveniently reached from Junction 9 on the M4 and along the A423 and A424, or from Junction 4 on the M40. Park in the car park adjoining the Sports Centre, which can easily be found by following the signs from near the river bridge, on the town side of it.

Leave the car park by walking towards the cricket field then bear left, keeping to the right of some iron railings until you nearly reach the towpath, then make towards a small bridge and cross it.

Before long we pass, on the other side of the river, Bisham's charming little waterside church with its twelfth century tower. There is a grim story told hereabouts of a certain Lady Hoby. An aunt of Francis Bacon, she lived in nearby Bisham Abbey and is said to have become so enraged with her clumsy and mentally-retarded son that she beat him to death for blotting his copybooks. Her monument may be seen in the church and her ghost at the Abbey. Oddly enough, some badly blotted and bloodstained sixteenth century copybooks were found in an attic by workmen renovating the Abbey some years ago, which seems to lend support to the legend.

On our side of the water, we cross a wooden footbridge over a tributary stream and, soon afterwards, two more little bridges. Beyond this point, wide views to distant hills open up ahead and to the right and left. This, indeed, is a wholly delightful stretch of the river Thames.

The next point of interest on the opposite bank is Bisham Abbey itself. Originally founded in the twelfth century, the present house is largely Tudor, built by Henry VIII and given to his fourth wife, Anne of Cleves. Now it is a Sports Council Centre for physical recreation and you will probably see activities ranging from canoeing to archery in progress over there.

Another little bridge takes us over another stream and then the path vanishes. But it does not matter, since our way still lies ahead beside the river, with soft grass now underfoot.

33

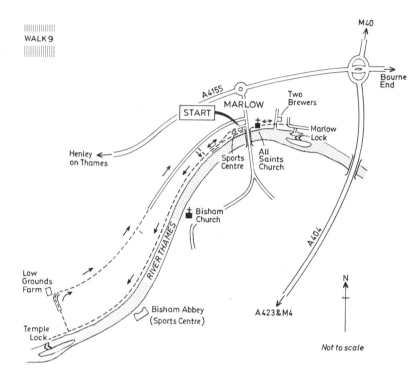

We cross a stile beside a cattle grid and, on coming abreast of Temple Island, cross yet another little bridge. Then the weirs of Temple Lock are in view. Just before we come level with the beginning of the first weir a cart track goes off to the right. Turn along here, but before doing so, you may care to go a little further beside the river for a closer look at the weirs and picturesque Temple Lock with its flower beds in a setting of chestnut trees.

The track (to which you have returned) comes to a tubular metal gate and then runs straight ahead between fields towards Low Grounds Farm. Just short of the farm we pass another metal gate with a small wooden one beside it and then, a few yards further along, reach another similar pair of gates on the right. Beyond them, where the main track bends left to the farmhouse, a rougher track curves round to the right. This is the way we go. The track runs clearly along the right-hand edge of a large field.

At the end of the field we cross a stile and once over it, find the path continuing through woodland before transforming itself into an asphalt lane which soon crosses a small bridge. On reaching a rough layby on the right, we turn right along a shady path. This brings us back to the riverside where we turn left to enjoy, as we walk, a good view of Marlow's famous suspension bridge, opened in 1832. William Tierney Clark, its designer, was an unlucky bridge builder for his Hammersmith Bridge was replaced in 1885, while his most famous work, the bridge that linked Buda with Pest, was destroyed in the war.

Soon the little bridge where we started our towpath walk is reached and we bear left across the grass. Now if you wish you can go back to the car park where you left your car, but I should like you first to come on a short, yet very interesting, walk to Marlow Lock through fascinating Seven Corner Alley.

Bear right in front of the Sports Centre. On reaching a children's play area, cut across the grass towards a small iron gate leading into the road almost opposite All Saints Church. Cross the road and go ahead, beside the churchyard wall until, just past the gate-posts (the gates are missing) a small path runs right beneath yew trees. The path curves left, now between walls, to emerge facing the Two Brewers, one of Marlow's most notable pubs. On the right-hand side of it the path, signposted to Marlow Lock, continues between walls.

The narrow path which we are following was used by bargemen bringing their towing horses from the lock to Marlow bridge. In those days, as now, there was no towpath between these points, in consequence of which a towing rope a quarter of a mile long was needed when the horse regained the riverside.

We come out into a quiet residential road and turn right for a few yards to the river, where the road bends left and a 'Public Footpath' sign points the way over a bridge to the lock. I think you will agree that the memorable view from the bridge — of river, weir, suspension bridge and church — makes this short diversion well worth while and is an ample reward for the necessity now to retrace our steps to the car park.

Walk 10   Hurley

5¼ miles (8.5 km)

OS sheet 175

A couple of paths on this walk could be found overgrown at certain seasons of the year. Lady walkers may therefore care to weigh the merits of jeans or trousers as offering the best protection against stinging nettles. Otherwise, this is an enjoyable ramble with easy gradients through pleasant countryside.

The starting point is Hurley, a village lying at the end of a minor road, signposted 'Hurley Village', which runs north from the A423 about four miles east of Henley by the side of a pub called The East Arms. Drive down this minor road as far as you can and park in a large, free car park on your left.

Our walk begins along a footpath, with a 'No Cycling' sign, beside the vehicle entrance to the car park. You may, however, first like to visit nearby St Mary's Church, an interesting-looking flint edifice with a wooden tower. It once formed part of Hurley Priory, founded in 1086 and dissolved by Henry VIII. To the left of the church is the gateway to the former monastery, now private property, while the Olde Bell Inn, which you passed in the car just now, is said to have been the monastery's guest house.

The path takes us to a flight of steps leading to a wooden footbridge. Go up the steps but do not cross the bridge, although it is worth going onto it for the view of nearby Hurley Lock. At the top of the steps turn left onto the Thames towpath. For the next few hundred yards the sound of water tumbling over the weirs comes over loudly from the other side of the river.

Level with the far end of the weirs, pass through a gate by a cattle grid and continue on the gravelled path which soon peters out, leaving us walking on grass. After a while we cross a stile the pattern of which will probably be as unfamiliar to you as it was to me.

Further along, a path comes in from a caravan site on the left and an iron gate lies ahead. Pass by it and continue on a small path at the waterside. The river broadens now to embrace three luxuriant islands and we pass another iron gate to continue along a small riverside road. Ignore a 'Public Footpath' sign and soon, beyond double iron gates, we come to a road at Frogmill Farm. Turn left into this pleasant, narrow country road.

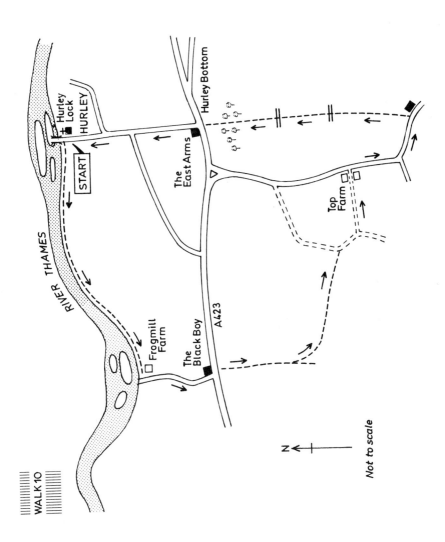

WALK 10

RIVER THAMES

Hurley Lock

HURLEY

START

The East Arms

Hurley Bottom

Frogmill Farm

The Black Boy

A423

Top Farm

N

Not to scale

37

In a quarter of a mile the A423 is reached, at a pub called The Black Boy. Turn left, for a few yards only. By the end of The Black Boy's buildings cross this busy, and fast, road carefully to a bridleway going up through the bushes. This is our way, and this is the first of the paths you may find a little overgrown. As it gently climbs, the noise of the traffic on the A423 fades and pleasant pastoral views open up. Ignore two stiles facing each other, left and right.

At the top of the hill carry on along the path ahead. Before long, two stone direction signs will be encountered on the left, one of them saying 'Public Bridleway to Honey Lane'. Take this route, through a truly delightful woodland glade, which is a nature reserve, and shortly you may spot one or two waymarks to reassure you that you have not strayed. Ignore a stile on the right by a bridleway sign, and leave the wood by a wooden gate.

Beyond this, the path soon becomes a cart track, offering wide views to the right over the neatly fenced fields of the Grassland Research Institute. The track merges with a concrete drive sweeping in from private property on the left, but continue ahead with a wire fence on the right until a fenced cart track comes in from the left, just before the drive curves slightly right towards a wood. Turn squarely left onto the cart track towards Top Farm which can be seen ahead.

Pass through the farm (it is a public right of way) and come out into a lane in which turn right. At a T-junction, turn left.

Just before reaching some red-brick houses, cross a stile on your left. The path ahead is not discernible on the ground but it runs close to the fence on the right of the big field and at the end of the field, in a slight dip, you will find a stile.

A single-plank bridge then crosses a ditch and brings you to another stile. In the field beyond the path may again not be plain on the ground, but fix your eye on the centre of the wood ahead in the distance and aim towards that point. You will come to a stile with footpath signs beside it. Cross the drive and a stile and take the path ahead through another large field, still making roughly for the mid-point of the wood. Go over a crossing path and soon cross a stile and pass through the wood, a wire fence on your left. The wood, although wide, turns out not to be deep and before long you are at a stile which leads into a path going straight ahead down the hill. This path, too, may be found somewhat overgrown towards the end.

At the foot of the hill you come out, over a stile at Hurley Bottom, onto the A423 again. Cross the road carefully and take the minor road through Hurley Village, passing The East Arms, The Rising Sun and The Olde Bell in the comparatively short distance before you reach your car.

Walk 11   Medmenham

8 miles (12.5 km)

OS sheet 175

This is not a beginner's walk, being longer than most walks in this book and more strenuous, since there are hills to be climbed. It is slightly adventurous, too, in that there are quite big and lonely woods to be passed through and obstacles such as fallen trees to be scrambled over. Yet it is a rewarding walk and the reach of the Thames covered is one of the loveliest of all.

About three miles from Henley on the A4155 towards Marlow, a minor road signposted 'Hambleden, Skirmett and Fingest' runs north. A quarter of a mile along this road, on the left, is a free car park. This is our starting point.

Leave the car park and turn right for a few yards only to a minor road on the left and immediately go left through a swing gate. The path follows the left edge of the field and comes, after about a third of a mile, to a swing gate leading into a rough lane just short of a little bridge. Cross the bridge and keep left when the lane forks. Look out for a gap in the hedge on the right after rather less than a quarter of a mile, where a waymarked path begins. Follow this path up the hill and through the wood, climbing all the way. Keep to the main path, ignoring all minor paths left and right, until you meet a waymarked crossing track near the top. Turn left, and after only a few yards go over a stile lying a short distance from the path, on your right. (Be careful not to miss it.)

The path then goes ahead, by the side of a wood at first and then straight across the field. At a hedge, the path becomes a track until a stile and gate are reached on the other side of a crossing track. Beyond the stile a grassy track brings us to a narrow road, in which we turn left.

When the road turns sharply left at a farm, carry on ahead by a footpath sign and over a stile, on the other side of which the path — not very visible here — runs at the right-hand edge of the field, with a wire fence on the right, to another stile. Beyond this, keeping to the 'invisible' path, go over the field to a stile you will soon see plainly against the dark trees behind it. Once over the stile, and then another, you are in a very pleasant leafy lane, where you should turn right.

Keep to the lane for about a quarter of an hour and at a junction of little roads by Brockmer End Farm carry on ahead for a short

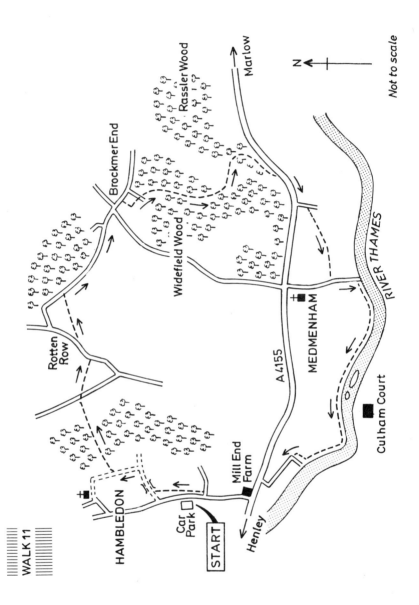

WALK 11

START

Car Park

HAMBLEDON

Mill End Farm

Henley

Rotten Row

Widefield Wood

Brockmer End

Rassler Wood

Marlow

A4155

MEDMENHAM

Culham Court

RIVER THAMES

N

Not to scale

40

distance on the road signposted 'Marlow'. At a footpath sign on your right just past a house called Widefield, a short length of path (overgrown maybe) takes us to a stile on the left, which we cross and go slightly right over a field to a stile near its far right corner. Cross a concrete drive (half-right) to a stile leading into Widefield Wood.

Now be a little careful. The path starts off more or less ahead, then forks rightwards, but look out for a waymark (a white-painted arrow) on a tree to point the way. Once you are on the path, waymarks will guide you all the way through this dark and, some may say, eerie wood. Eventually you leave the wood at a stile.

The path then follows the wire fence to the left and comes to a stile leading into a rough track. Opposite, another stile leads into another wood. This time there are no waymarks to guide us but the path is plain enough, and it keeps pretty near to the right-hand edge of the wood and climbs for a while. Towards the end it bends left and, after passing two stiles, comes out into a drive in which we turn left to the A4155.

Turn right. There is now an unavoidable, but short, stretch of road walking, although there is a pavement of sorts for part of the way and it is downhill. Follow, after rather less than a third of a mile, a footpath sign on the left pointing down a drive to Abbey Lodge. Beyond the second of two small bridges an iron gate on the right marks the start of a path to a stile. Beyond, the path across the field is quite invisible, which makes the instruction on a nearby notice board, 'Keep Strictly to Footpath', easier to say than to obey. Nevertheless, if you head towards the left-hand side of a corral-type fence round a wooden building you can see ahead you won't go far wrong. Lying back from the corner of the fence is a waymarked stile, a wooden footbridge and a clear path ahead at the right-hand edge of a wood. The path leads out to a pleasant, small road by Monks Cottage at Medmenham. Turn left towards the river Thames and turn right along the towpath.

A mile and a half of sheer delight lie ahead. This is indeed a lovely reach of the river, with glorious views on either side. There is little, however, for me to point out to you apart from Culham Court, a splendid redbrick mansion of 1770, which you will not fail to notice anyway. I will therefore leave you to enjoy your walk until the towpath abruptly ends where it is cut off by the garden of a white, thatched house. Turn right here and make your way beside a hedge up the left-hand side of a field, at the end of which there is a stile on the left leading into a drive. Carry on ahead along the long, straight drive to the A4155 road. Turn left for a short distance and then, just past Mill End Farm, turn right into the road in which the car park lies.

5¼ or 3 miles (8.5 or 5 km)

OS sheet 175

Special note On Henley Royal Regatta days, in July, there is no right of way along most of the towpath between Remenham and Henley. At that time, therefore, it may be possible only to undertake the shorter walk of 3 miles.

A pleasant walk through wide fields and meadows, along an attractive reach of the river with a sight of picturesque old Hambleden Mill, an adventurous trip across a turbulent weir as an optional extra, and — for those undertaking the longer walk — a little something that will surely bring a lump to the throat of any dog-lover.

The hamlet of Remenham, the starting point of our walk, can be reached down either of two small signposted roads running north from the A423. One of them, Remenham Lane, leaves the main road just to the east of Henley bridge by the Little Angel Hotel. The other, which you will come to first if you are approaching from the London/Maidenhead direction, is signposted 'Remenham Church' and it leaves the A423 the second turning after it begins the steep descent down Remenham Hill into Henley. It should not be difficult to park near Remenham church.

Remenham church, which you may care to visit before you set off, is dedicated to St Nicholas, better known as Santa Claus. There has been a church here since before 1066 but nineteenth century restorations, alas, eliminated most of the ancient building. We start our walk by taking the road to the right of the church and when it soon forks, take the right fork signposted 'Maidenhead'. The road climbs quite steeply for a while, giving good views over the wide meadows to the river and Temple Island, and then it curves to the right. At the end of the curve a track, signposted 'Public Footpath', goes off to the left. Follow this track, with great rolling fields on either side at first, for half a mile.

Now be a little careful. At the point where the track turns sharply left and becomes a rough lane (by a double 6-bar iron gate on the right) go straight ahead by a tiny path. The first few yards may be somewhat overgrown. Follow the rather faint path through a field and come out into a small road by Highway Cottage. Turn left down the road to the Flower Pot Inn.

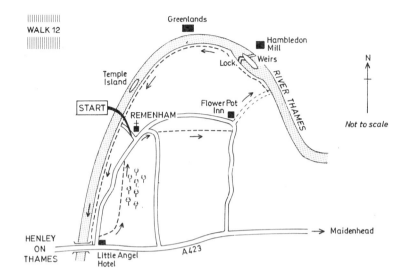

Take the road to the right of the inn and soon you reach the river. Turn left over a footbridge and proceed with the river on your right. There is, at first, no path to speak of but you can't go wrong. After a short half mile the famous white weatherboarded sixteenth century Hambleden Mill, which worked until 1958, will be seen on the opposite bank and soon Hambleden lock and its weirs, a most impressive sight, comes into view.

When you reach the lock you can, if you wish, go over to Hambleden Mill along a narrow footbridge which crosses the weirs. The rushing water beneath makes this quite an experience. It is safe, although children, needless to say, must be kept under control.

When you return from your expedition across the weirs, continue the walk past the lock, still keeping to the riverside. The path, you will notice, changes its character from time to time, being sometimes narrow, sometimes broad, occasionally made up and often non-existent. We pass, in a landscape adorned with decorative trees, on the opposite bank, a beautiful house called Greenlands, which was built by a Victorian First Lord of the Admiralty, W.H. Smith, a son of the newsagent of the same name. It is now the Administrative Staff College. Then we come to luxuriant Temple Island which we saw in the distance soon after we started our walk. At the far end of the island is a curious cottage with a cupola that gives the island its name.

43

Soon after passing the island we reach a point where there is a low wall on the left, then a stile and a wide double iron gate beside it and the towing path ahead crosses a narrow cattle grid. *For the shorter walk*, cross the stile and take the walled lane the short distance up into Remenham, where you left your car.

For the longer walk, cross the cattle grid or the stile beside it and carry on along the towing path. The boathouses of Henley and the church tower beyond can now be seen ahead. Ignore a footpath sign you shortly pass indicating a path leading away from our route, which continues at the waterside. We pass the U.T.R.C. boathouse, the Remenham Club clubhouse and several footbridges and gates as we gradually approach Henley bridge. This is the reach of the river that comes alive during Henley's famous regatta week.

Just before Henley bridge, by the Leander Club, the path swings away to the left and brings us to the busy A423 road — but only for a few yards. Turn left and very shortly leave the main road by going left into quiet Remenham Lane. About 200 yards along it, just after passing The Home Farm entrance, a 'Public Footpath' sign on the right points our way over a stile. Go towards and then through a small gap in the trees ahead and then half-left over a golf course, a footpath sign indicating the direction, although the path is barely discernible. At the far side a narrow path leads up through the trees.

Before entering this path, however, don't fail to pause to read the touching inscription on a small tablet erected to the memory of a much-loved 'little dog with a big heart' named Minty, who used to await his mistress at this spot and who died in 1970.

Cross the stile ahead and take the earth path half-left through the trees. It goes between hawthorn bushes along a hillside and can be slippery in wet weather but it improves after a short distance. When the hawthorn bushes end, continue with a fence on the left. Cross a stile and carry on with the fence still on the left. Cross another stile by a 6-bar iron gate. The way now becomes a cart track and drops down into Remenham Lane. Turn right for a short half mile along this delightful leafy lane, with the river below on the left, and you will soon find yourself back in Remenham where you left your car.

7 miles (11 km)

OS sheet 175

'In every English woodland you can hear the music of Delius', wrote Beverley Nichols (who else?). If that is so, you will hear his music today for our walk passes through several small, but very lovely, woods. The starting point is Shiplake, which lies on the A4155 Reading to Henley-on-Thames road about 2½ miles from the latter. Look out for a pub called The Plowden Arms and turn into a minor road signposted 'Binfield Heath and Peppard' beside it. There is another road similarly signposted but the one you want is the one alongside the pub. Park in a small layby opposite Plowden Way or in another a few yards further along.

Start walking along the road away from the main road. Pass a couple of turnings and Memorial Avenue and soon turn into a stony lane on the right. It is straight at first and bordered by trees, but when the lane eventually bends sharply left we carry on through a squeeze stile and along a cart track ahead, with glorious views to the right.

After a while the track enters Shiplake Woods. Keep to the main track running ahead and, shortly, downhill. Ignore all the tracks leading off to the left and right and keep always to the main one. The track ends when the wood ends. A path then runs clearly ahead across a field towards another wood (Harpsden Wood), but we do not enter it yet. Instead, when we emerge at the end of the field into a drive, we turn left along it and, as the drive narrows, pass a sign saying 'Private Road, Public Footpath'. Past Ash Farm, our way bends right, then left, and continues beneath trees.

On coming to a stile on the right, just before the path divides, cross it and follow a path, half-right, along the right-hand edge of the field to another stile. Another stile is now seen straight ahead across the next field and, over this, yet another in the corner of the field in front.

On the other side of the last of these stiles we follow the stony lane opposite. Ignore all forks to the left and right and forge ahead on the main track until — be a little careful here — you reach a fork on the left signposted to 'Harpsden Wood House' and 'Harpsden Wood Cottage'. Here, bear half-right onto a waymarked path through the woods. Cross a minor road and carry on along the waymarked path

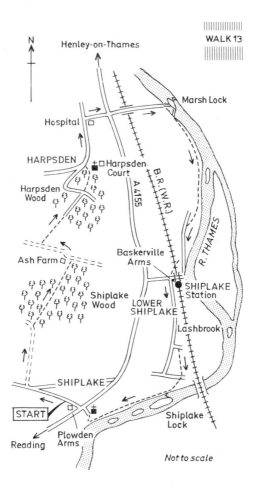

opposite, maintaining your previous direction.

The path drops gradually towards the hamlet of Harpsden. The first things you will notice in Harpsden are the curious facings on three barns opposite the church which are old wooden blocks used in the printing of wallpaper.

Past the church and Harpsden Court, we bend left with the road, which begins as a pleasant enough country road at first but becomes residential later. However, it is not very far to the Henley War Memorial Hospital entrance where we turn right onto a bridleway beside it. This runs downhill and comes out into Waterman's Road, which leads ahead to the A4155. Cross, half-right, to Mill Lane.

This goes past the Sports Centre, over a railway bridge and comes to the river Thames.

Now begins quite an exciting adventure. A long wooden causeway takes us over the swirling, white-frothed water that has tumbled over the weir and brings us to Marsh Lock. No doubt you will wish to rest here for a while before setting off past the lock and across an even longer causeway which takes us back again to the bank we left earlier. We now start our towpath walk.

This is a delightful reach of the river. You will notice from time to time some iron studs by the side of the path. They were put there in 1903 to mark the 14 foot width of the towpath but through bank erosion, the bane of river and canal alike, the water's edge has crept very close to some of them. Near the end of the meadow, where the river splits into three channels, the towpath changes sides, but since the ferry has long gone we must leave the riverside for a while. A wooden footbridge leads to a stile and a path which merges with a rough drive. Soon, at a kissing gate, a small sign indicates a footpath running between two drives.

When the footpath ends, we carry on along a road ahead and when it forks we keep left. Opposite a house called Eyot Wood, we fork half-right along what begins as a delightful grassy path between hedges and comes to an iron kissing gate and a stile leading onto the railway. Cross carefully to the other side where a path brings us up to a road junction at the Baskerville Arms.

Carry on along Mill Road opposite and through the hamlet of Lashbrook for nearly half a mile, then turn left into the drive of the British Red Cross Society's Andrew Duncan House. A few yards along, negotiate a steep stile on the right and cross the corner of a field to another stile. Turn right along the right-hand edge of a field and come out into a lane by picturesque Mill House. Turn right, then immediately left onto a footpath to Shiplake Lock and we reach the river again.

You can go over the footbridge to view the lock at closer quarters if you wish, but return and cross the stile to the towpath. Another beautiful reach of the river lies before us, a scene of tree-lined banks, tiny islands and sloping meadows. Through gates and over stiles and a small footbridge, our towpath walk brings us after rather more than half a mile to a point below Shiplake College.

Do not cross the footbridge ahead but take the path which runs behind a boathouse and then, just when it *almost* meets another path on the left, curves round right and climbs to Shiplake Church. Alfred, Lord Tennyson, was married here on 13 June 1850, and a poem (not one of his best) which he wrote that day is on sale in the church.

Turn left (west) along the lane and come out to the A4155 almost opposite the Plowden Arms near our starting point.

5½ miles (9 km)

OS sheet 175

A very pleasant, easy excursion on paths that range from good to excellent. Our walk begins and ends in Pangbourne, which is on the A329 about six miles west of Reading, but more specifically, our starting point is the car park between The Copper Inn and the railway station.

At the roundabout in front of The Copper Inn take the road signposted 'Reading' towards the shops and almost at once turn into Whitchurch Road by The George ('Established before 1295', it says). Just before reaching the Victorian toll bridge drop down, right, to the towpath and turn right. We are now on Pangbourne Meadow.

You are probably wondering why we are walking downstream when all the other walks in this book are upstream. The answer is that it is for only half a mile or so and we shall finish our walk on this same stretch of towpath in the 'proper' direction.

We cross two stiles and come to a small concrete footbridge over a tributary stream and another stile. We cross and immediately turn right onto a path running beside the stream and which keeps near it all the way to the railway. Instead of passing through the bridge under the line we turn left to follow a path running close to the foot of the embankment.

Neither do we go through another small railway bridge we shortly reach, but instead maintain our previous direction beside the embankment. Soon the main path bends left, with a wire fence on the right and pointing directly towards a smooth green hill in the distance ahead. The path bends right at the corner of the fence and heads towards the right-hand side of Scraces Farm, soon broadening out to become a wide grassy track with a sturdy wooden fence.

Past a double wooden gate, we carry on along the narrow farm road, turning right when it joins the little road from Westbury Farm. Immediately before the road crosses the railway, however, we turn left along a path with a wire fence on either side and the railway below on the right. You may notice — indeed you may well trip over them — some old iron boundary markers along the path with the inscription 'Great Western Railway Co. Boundary 1890'.

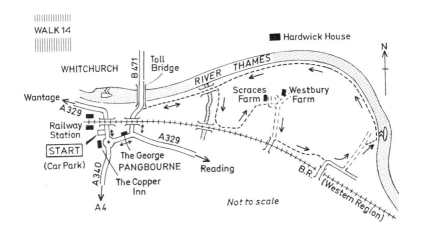

We come to a bridge on the right over the railway and a triple footpath/bridleway sign on the left. Carry on ahead, maintaining the previous direction, but almost at once the path — now a bridleway — bears slightly left. It curves and eventually emerges into a road at a corner and we turn left along the road signposted 'Purley Village'. Just before the road ends, we turn left along Mapledurham Drive at a 'Public Footpath' sign.

After passing an iron gate across our way the drive becomes a gravel track as it passes a recreation ground called Bucknell's Meadow. When another gate bars our way we do not go through it but to its right, over the field towards the weir which can be seen ahead.

On reaching the towpath, turn left through a gate to Mapledurham Lock (a prize-winning lock), pass beside it and out through a gate at the other end. Now begins a wholly delightful couple of miles of Thames-side walking. Look out for Hardwick House on the other side of the water. This fine old gabled mansion dates back to Tudor times — and Queen Elizabeth I slept here, 'tis said — but parts were rebuilt following damage in the Civil War.

You can put this book away now if you like for you cannot get lost. You will eventually come to the footbridge over the tributary stream which you crossed earlier on and then you will know where you are. Follow the length of towpath through Pangbourne Meadow, in the 'correct' direction this time, and then you will be back in the town where you left your car.

8 miles (13 km)

OS sheet 175

Although this is one of our longer walks, and more strenuous than most, it is very rewarding and our efforts in climbing the hills are repaid with some marvellous views. We start and finish in Goring, an attractive riverside town which is perhaps most easily reached from the A329, the Reading to Wallingford road, by turning on to the B4009 at Streatley.

Park in the public car park or in the railway station car park (follow the signs) and then make your way to the Reading road (B4526), which starts by the bridge over the railway, and turn with it at the Queen's Arms. The second little road we come to on the right is Whitehills Green. Enter it, go left as it bends, then right at the island and then along a hedged path to a stile. Go over a large, smooth playing field, half-left, to a stile in its far corner.

Cross the stile and turn sharp left along the left-hand edge of the field. Here we start climbing quite steeply, but splendid views open up. At a stile, the path flattens out and deteriorates, but it can still be followed along the left-hand edge of the next field. On meeting a barbed wire fence the path bends right and, in the corner of the field, comes to another stile and, within a few yards, to yet another which takes us into Great Chalk Wood.

Follow the clear path, which you may find a little overgrown for a while. Ignore forks to the right and left through fire-breaks which we reach fairly soon, and carry on ahead. The path now becomes much wider and is not overgrown. When it bends a little to the left ignore another path going off to the right and come to a good crossing track. Our way here lies ahead along a wide, shady earth track which leads right when another track joins it from the left, at a gate.

You may find this track, which climbs gently, a little muddy for a while. (I have never understood how water can lie on a slope.) Near the top of the hill we come to a T-junction of tracks and turn left to a gate and the remains of a stile by a notice saying 'Sporting reserved', and carry on along the main path beyond the gate, ignoring a small path to the right. Our path ends at a field gate. Go through this and across the paddock leftwards to another gate leading into a

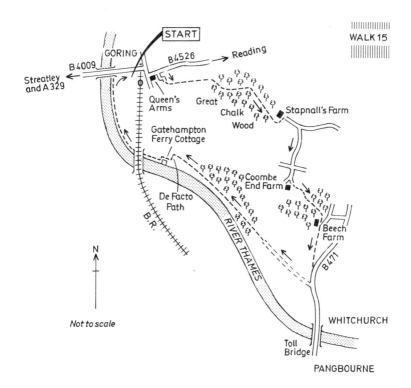

START

GORING

Reading

B4526

B4009

Streatley
and A329

Queen's
Arms

Great
Chalk
Wood

Stapnall's Farm

Gatehampton
Ferry Cottage

Coombe
End Farm

De Facto
Path

B.R.

RIVER THAMES

Beech
Farm

B471

N

Not to scale

WHITCHURCH

Toll
Bridge

PANGBOURNE

narrow lane, with Stapnalls Farm to the left. This farm, the farmer told me, stands on the site of a thirteenth century nunnery.

Turn right along the lane and shortly go right into another lane which leads into a small road. The drive opposite is signposted 'Public Footpath. Whitchurch 1 mile', and this is the way we go. Follow the drive, bearing left when it forks and then, just short of the farm buildings, cross a stile on the left. The path, not very visible on the ground, skirts the buildings on the right and comes to a small stile (easily missed) in the fence on the right. It is not far beyond the last of the buildings. Cross it and go half-left across the field to a small stile in the barbed wire fence. Then take your bearings so as to maintain your direction across the next field towards the wood ahead and a stile leading into it.

Over the stile the path through the wood goes *straight ahead*. Ignore crossing paths and carry on ahead, the path weaving left and right a little at times. Go through an iron kissing gate and a paddock, a barbed wire fence on the right, and come out through another kissing gate at Beech Farm.

On the opposite side of the drive yet another kissing gate leads into a wide, grassy track which skirts the farm. When the track ends

51

our way runs plainly at the right-hand edge of a field all the way to the B471 road. Turn right for a few steps to the curiously isolated Whitchurch war memorial and cross the road there, for at this point an elevated path commences enabling us to avoid walking on the road itself. When the path ends you will see a signpost saying 'Public Bridleway. Goring 3 miles' and indicating a bridleway on the other side of the road. Turn into this bridleway which soon starts gently to climb.

After a mile, when the main track turns sharply left to Hartslock Farm, we go ahead on a footpath, a barbed wire fence on our right, and drop steeply downhill into a valley and then steeply up the other side. At a notice saying 'Private Woodland. No Shooting. Keep to Arrowed Path' we enter a wood and, of course, the arrows painted on the trees make it difficult for us to lose our way. Suddenly — delightful surprise — we find ourselves at an astonishing viewpoint. The ground falls precipitously at our feet and there below is the Thames, an unexpected and breathtaking sight.

The path now runs along a wooded terrace high above the river with glorious views beyond it, and then begins slowly to descend. When the woodland ends the path continues, with fields and hills to the right and the tree-lined river to the left. Soon you will see, over to your left, Gatehampton Ferry Cottage, which marks the point where the towpath begins on this side of the water. At the time of writing it seems to be necessary, in order to reach the towpath, to take a *de facto* path which may be subject to alteration. You are accordingly advised to heed any new route-signs, diversion signs or waymarks. My route was to cross a stile on the left, a couple of hundred yards or so short of a white house, to cross a small field and then a wire fence and a stile to reach a narrow path running right, a few feet from the river's edge. This leads to a tiny footbridge by the cottage where one turns right onto the towpath. An overgrown section ends at a stile, beyond which we skirt a summer-time camping site and pass beneath a railway bridge.

We are now in the lovely Goring Gap where the Chilterns and the Berkshire Downs once probably joined until the river bored and eroded a new way through for itself. Carry on at the water's edge — although sometimes the path takes a short cut when the river meanders — and eventually we reach Goring Bridge, with Goring lock and weir beyond. Turn right beside the bridge past an old water mill, up onto the road and into the town. Your car is not far away.

7¼ miles (11.5 km)

OS sheets 174 and 175

This is a walk on which we are rewarded with wide panoramic views. Of necessity, therefore, there are hills to be climbed which means that today's expedition is more strenuous than some. Nevertheless, it is not all that strenuous and no particular difficulties are likely to be encountered. Also, it is especially interesting because as well as following the Thames towpath we tread two other notable pathways. One is the Ridgeway Path, an officially-designated walkers' route, which for most of its length follows ancient trackways that were here when the Romans came. The other is the Icknield Way, the oldest prehistoric trackway in England.

The starting point is the village of South Stoke, which lies just off the B4009, the road running north from Goring to meet the A4074 near Crowmarsh Gifford, just across the bridge from Wallingford. It is quite easy to park, discreetly of course, in the village.

Near the end of the road towards the river take a lane signposted 'Ridgeway Path' and 'To the River'. On coming to the river, at a point where the Beetle and Wedge ferry formerly crossed, turn right through a gate onto the towpath. There are pleasant, if not sensational, views all around while ahead is the sturdy Moulsford railway bridge. As we pass beneath it we realise that here is yet another masterpiece created by the genius of Isambard Kingdom Brunel, the engineer of the Great Western Railway. Built in 1840, its diagonal brick courses make pleasing patterns and the effect, as one stands beneath it, is strangely impressive.

We pass two small tree-covered islands and the scenery seems to change in a subtle way. It changes again as we cross a footbridge and trees encroach almost to the water's edge. But soon we come to Little Stoke where the towpath switches sides. Since, however, we have missed the last ferry by several decades we must take another route a little way inland.

Turn right along the ferry lane (it is signposted 'Ridgeway Path') for about 20 yards and then left along a path signposted 'Ridgeway Path' and 'Public Footpath to North Stoke'. A stile brings us into a field, the left-hand edge of which we follow, with the river not far

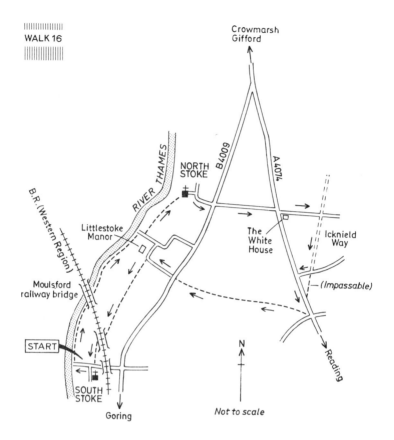

away to our left. Over a little concrete footbridge and a stile, and then another stile at the opposite side of a field, the path continues at the left-hand edge of yet another field. At the end of it a stile leads to a path which takes us through woodland to another stile giving onto a grassy area with North Stoke's thirteenth century St Mary's Church to the right. A stile brings us into the churchyard. The church is notable for some fourteenth century wall paintings.

Through the lych gate and along a short lane we turn right through the village and then bear left with the road. A little more than a mile of tarmac lies ahead, I am afraid, yet as it is a quiet country road with hardly any traffic and offering wide views it is by no means unpleasant. We reach the B4009 and cross to the very minor road opposite signposted 'Ipsden and Stoke Row'. This leads to the A4074 on which we jink right and then left to follow the 'Ipsden and Stoke Row' signpost pointing to the left of a pub called The White House. As this pleasant little road gently climbs we soon see, silhouetted against the sky, a 'Public Bridleway' sign on each side of the road. Turn onto the bridleway on the right.

This is the Icknield Way. Probably about 4,000 years old, it starts at Avebury in Wiltshire and extends, some experts believe, to Norfolk, following the highest ground possible to avoid low-lying marsh areas, wolves and other dangers. The going is good until we reach a lane. Then, alas, the way ahead is so hopelessy overgrown that a short diversion is necessary. Turn right along the lane to the A4074 on which turn left, and fortunately there are grassy tracks to walk on on the right-hand side.

After a short distance turn right into a minor road signposted 'South Stoke and Goring' and, almost at once, onto a lovely bridleway, signposted 'Little Stoke', which winds most invitingly up and over the hill. On its crest glorious panoramic views open up all around. To the right lies Wallingford, where William the Conqueror and his army, with insurrections to quell, forded the Thames. On the hilltop to the left of the town the tall beeches of Wittenham Clumps can be easily picked out, marking the site of an ancient hill fort, probably Iron Age.

As our path drops to some farm buildings and then begins to climb again towards a copse, its quality underfoot improves considerably. It emerges eventually onto the B4009. We cross, and go ahead along a narrow road signposted to 'Little Stoke' and, where the road bends right, climb over a stone stile to the left of the entrance gates to Littlestoke Manor.

Invisibly at first, the path runs at the right-hand edge of a field and crosses a stile and a footbridge. It then weaves clearly across the next field before it bends right, then left, and passes through a tunnel under the railway. It turns left on the other side then goes half-right across a field, then left towards the houses of South Stoke. We enter the village opposite Manor Farm, behind which lies the church where Cromwell stabled his horses during the siege of Wallingford, and turn right down the village street towards wherever the car is parked.

2½ **miles (4 km)**

OS sheet 175

This walk was planned to be longer than it is for I intended to take you along the towpath as far as Benson Lock. But this scheme was thwarted when I found that the path has been seriously eroded in the last half mile or so. So I curtailed my intended itinerary, leaving us with what is little more than a gentle stroll, although quite a pleasant and interesting one.

On the Crowmarsh Gifford side of Wallingford Bridge is a public open space with various recreational amenities in a field given in memory of the son of a prominent Wallingford family who was killed in the war. Park in the car park there.

As you make your way up the slope back to the road, glance beneath the bridge and notice how it was widened (although it is narrow enough still) at some time in the past. The arches are rounded on this side while on the other side the original pointed arches can be seen.

Cross the road, half-left, to a stile with a footpath sign at the end of the parapet opposite and then go half-left across the small field to an iron kissing gate. Our way now follows the right-hand edge of a field with a barbed wire fence on the right until, at the end of the field, we cross a crude bridge to a stile. The path then continues towards a farm ahead.

As we approach the farm a wide path appears between a red-brick house and the farm buildings, curving round in front of us towards a double stile and a small bridge on the right. Go over these.

The Thames lies ahead. We make towards it and turn right. Although the map shows the path as running a little distance inland from the river, barbed wire ahead and the absence of a bridge across a stream clearly mean that the *de facto* path is where one would expect it to be, beside the water. Pass through a grey-painted gate and over a pleasant meadow towards Wallingford Bridge which, it is plain to see from here, has been altered and added to during its 700-year history. The ancient town with its three churches forms a backcloth to the river. (Once there were fourteen churches, before the Black Death in 1348 wiped out the population until only 44 families remained.)

A wooden footbridge and a stile bring us into a small meadow

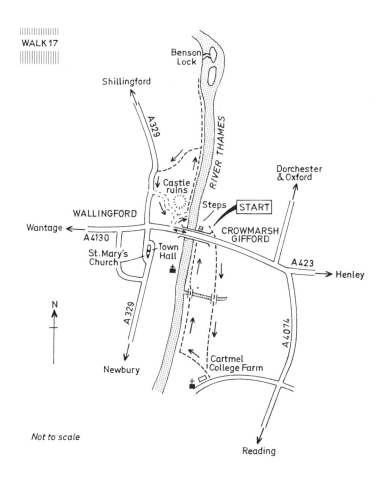

Benson
Lock

Shillingford

A329

RIVER THAMES

Dorchester
& Oxford

Castle
ruins

Steps

START

WALLINGFORD

Wantage ←

A4130

CROWMARSH
GIFFORD

St. Mary's
Church

Town
Hall

A423

Henley

N

A329

A4074

Newbury

Cartmel
College Farm

Reading

Not to scale

and we then pass beneath the bridge, through the arch nearest to the river. On the other side of the bridge an elegant flight of steps takes us up onto the carriageway and we turn right towards the town. Beside the Town Arms at the end of the bridge, however, we turn right into a lane and then right again towards the waterside then left along the towpath.

In a moment or two, to the left, can be seen the now insignificant remains of Wallingford Castle, once one of the largest in the land. Built by the Normans on the site of a Roman fort it was a stronghold that survived many an assault until at last it was destroyed in the Civil War. As the castle drops behind us we cross a wooden footbridge and carry on beside the river, now with iron railings on the left.

We come to a stile on the left and cross it. Here, reluctantly,

57

we must leave the riverside because of the eroded state of the towpath ahead. Cross the meadow, with iron railings on the left. We pass by a 6-bar tubular iron gate, cross a rough track and a stile into a hedged track in which we turn left. Another view of the castle ruins is afforded as the track bends right and leads into the Shillingford road (A329). Cross to the pavement opposite and turn left. We do not stay on the road for long, however, for soon after it has bent right, then left, we turn down (beside a house numbered 24) a narrow, walled lane.

This curious and quite fascinating bit of old Wallingford— undiscovered by most of the town's visitors, I'll warrant—seems to me to be an ancient road that once hugged the castle's outer wall. We go through a tunnel, bend right at a farm and emerge into the main road at the foot of the bridge.

Turn right if you wish to explore the town, which has numerous fine houses, some of which date from the sixteenth century, and a seventeenth century town hall in the square.

Or go left over the bridge. Pause as you cross it and turn to visualise in your mind's eye the great castle as it once was, occupying a vast area to your left. And recall that after it fell to Fairfax in the Civil War (it was one of the last Royalist strongholds to surrender). Oliver Cromwell, one day in 1646, watched from the bridge where you are now standing the execution of the whole of the defeated garrison. Their heads and decapitated bodies were hurled into the river. They doubtless bumped against the arches beneath us as they were borne away on the sanguined stream.

A gruesome thought to take with you back to the car.

Walk 18   Little Wittenham

5¾ or 5 miles (9.25 or 8 km)

OS sheet 164

An opportunity to visit historic Dorchester-on-Thames is one of the
features of this easy walk. The only difficulty might be a little mud
encountered in one or two places. We start and finish at Little
Wittenham, which is reached by taking a minor road signposted
'Wittenhams' running north from the A4130 between Wallingford
and Didcot and then turning right onto an even more minor road
signposted 'Little Wittenham'. Keep ahead when the road forks and
park near the church.

Just before the church, and on the other side of the road, is a stile.
Climb over and make your way slightly leftwards across the field
towards Little Wittenham Wood — *not* towards Wittenham Clumps,
the group of trees marking a possibly Iron Age hill fort on the rounded
hill in front. The path, not very visible on the ground at first,
gradually becomes more apparent and you will soon see a stile and
small gate leading into the wood. As you climb, there is a fine view of
the river Thames and Day's Lock and weir.

A grassy track goes through the wood, which has a wide variety of
trees, particularly cypress. When the track splits take the left fork,
maintaining your forward direction, and after a while the track
broadens out and starts slowly to descend. We finally leave the wood
by a small wooden gate and go forward on the left-hand side of a
large field enjoying good views all around. Soon the buildings of
North Farm appear.

The path ends and our way continues along a rough lane.
It passes North Farm and at this point the river comes into sight again,
away to the left. The lane soon jinks right and left and in another ten
minutes or so the A329 is reached at the Shillingford Bridge Hotel,
a welcome prospect, perhaps.

Turn left across the graceful Shillingford Bridge, which was built in
1830 and is clearly more suited to horse-drawn carriages and carts
than the cars and lorries that thunder over it today. But after only a
few yards we can thankfully escape the traffic down a drive to the left,
with a 'Public Footpath' sign, opposite Ferry House. When the drive
divides take the right fork and immediately enter a footpath. Just past
the wall of Shillingford Court a short path to the left leads down to

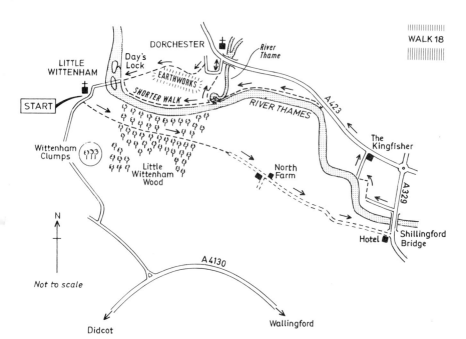

the riverside. Once upon a time, no doubt, this peaceful spot was busy with barges, for the road behind is called Wharf Road.

Regrettably, a short detour is now necessary since there is no right of way beside the next stretch of river. So go up pleasant, grass-bordered Wharf Road, admire the gorgeous wisteria that gives Wisteria Cottage its name, and come out on the A423 by the Kingfisher pub. An unavoidable six or seven minutes' walk, left, on this busy road now lies before us, I am afraid, but fortunately there is a pavement on the right-hand side.

Look out for a stile beside an iron gate on the left which will enable us to cross a field and reach the towpath. Turn right on the towpath and make your way, through meadows, along a pleasant reach of the river until you come to the footbridge (No. 167) over the river Thame, where it enters the Thames. If you do not wish to visit Dorchester, carry on beside the Thames (a lovely stretch) until you reach the Little Wittenham footbridge just before Day's Lock and skip the next three paragraphs.

The rest of us fork right immediately after crossing the Thame and follow its bank round in almost a semi-circle. Then follow the path as it heads across the field to a stile. Beyond it, you pass on the left some ancient earthworks known as the Dyke Hills, defences probably

60

dating from the Iron Age, and come to another stile. Cross, and turn right along the edge of a field. This brings us into a rough lane and soon we join a small road running in front of the Chequers Inn. Turn left. A tunnel by the public conveniences will take us safely under the main road to the entrance to the Abbey.

I will leave you now to explore the marvellous Abbey (it is said that money ran out before a nineteenth century 'restoration' was far advanced so relatively little harm was done) and the ancient small town. You follow in the footsteps of the Romans, the Saxons and of St Birinus, a missionary who came from Rome in AD635 and helped to make this place as important a Christian centre, at one time, as Canterbury. There is no shortage of refreshment places in Dorchester. The attractive George Inn is believed to have been the Abbey brewhouse in monastic times.

Those who knew Dorchester before the recently-opened bypass diverted the heavy traffic that used to shatter its single street will be delighted with the peace and quiet now regained by this historic town.

When you are ready to resume your walk, make your way back to the Chequers Inn and turn right along Watling Lane. Soon, a sign on the *right* saying 'Public Footpath to Day's Lock' points to a footpath on the *left*. Take this path, which runs towards the earthworks and, on reaching them, turn right. Pass over a crossing track. At a 5-bar gate the path bears left between fences. This enchanting path goes through a gate and forward to a footbridge we can see ahead, past Day's Lock on the right.

Once over the footbridge there are two more bridges to cross before going up a slight slope and round the corner. And there, by Little Wittenham Church, your car awaits.

Walk 19   Clifton Hampden

2½ **miles (4 km)**

OS sheet 164

The starting point of this short, though interesting, walk is the free car park at Clifton Hampden, a picturesque village full of picture-book thatched cottages and lying on the A415 between Dorchester and Abingdon. In the village, turn off the main road onto the minor Little Wittenham road, cross the narrow bridge and park in the car park on the left just round the bend.

Leave the car park and turn right past the Barley Mow and towards the bridge. This ancient inn, which bears the date 1352, was damaged by fire but restoration has been exquisitely accomplished. The inn is a remarkable example of visible cruck construction and was made famous by Jerome K. Jerome who, in *Three Men in a Boat*, described it as 'the quaintest, most old world inn up the river'.

The bridge, spanning the Thames, is remarkable too, but as it can best be seen from the riverside, cross over it and drop down the little path to the left on the other side and then turn right on the towpath. The bridge, as you will see, is, in its small way, worthy to stand beside Balmoral and the Houses of Parliament as an example of Medieval/Victorian design. Sir Gilbert Scott, no less, was responsible for it. It was paid for by a local family and replaced a ferry.

For a short distance, a caravan site on the opposite bank somewhat mars the view but thereafter our whole route is through very pleasant, if unsensational, countryside.

Just before we reach Clifton Lock you will notice the divergence of the natural river from the artificial Clifton Cut, which is now the navigation channel. For the rest of the waterside section of this ramble we shall have the impression of walking beside a canal, as indeed we are. There is no means of following the river's old course. We pass, but do not cross, a footbridge obviously built to enable the farmer to reach his fields cut off by the construction of the cut.

We reach the end of the artificial cut at the point at which the water tumbles over a weir into the original channel. Alas, we must leave the waterside here by turning right across the grass to a small iron gate beside a large one and follow a track running at a right angle to the river. Soon we pass another similar pair of gates — and then another, with a crossing track immediately after.

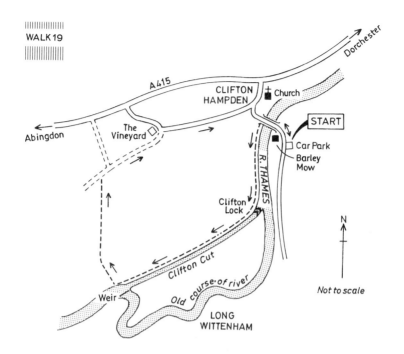

Beyond here our track, now much broader — and waymarked — goes half-right. At the end of the field the track bends right and its surface improves. Ignore, after a while, a track going left and continue ahead, the now gravelled way becoming a concrete farm road as we pass farm buildings and approach a fine weatherboarded house. Behind it, a surprising sight on this side of the Channel, is a vineyard.

We meet a small road at a corner and bear right. This wholly delightful road, with its grassy verges and thatched cottages, soon brings us to a road junction where we turn right a few yards to the bridge and the car park.

Before taking this turn, however, it is well worth while going ahead the short distance to the church of St Michael and All Angels, now much restored, which can be seen ahead perched high on a rock outcrop. It is approached up a long flight of steep steps which must surely deter elderly and arthritic worshippers but which nevertheless affords the hale and hearty a remarkable view of the river.

Walk 20 {#walk-20}   Culham

3½ miles (5.5 km)

OS sheet 164

Although this is quite a short walk it is not only full of interest and beauty but manages to straddle two counties, for we visit Culham in Oxfordshire and Sutton Courtenay in Berkshire.

Culham, our starting point, lies about two miles south of Abingdon at a junction of three minor roads, two of which run from the Abingdon/Dorchester road (A415) and the other from the B4016. Park discreetly by Culham church, which you will find near the end of a little road that crosses the village green from beside The Lion pub. The Manor House, which you will see opposite the church, is one of the two exceptional houses this small village boasts; the other is the Georgian Culham House, which can be seen beyond the green through its fine wrought iron gates, a splendidly proportioned edifice.

From the church make your way back to the road where, at a corner of the green, the village pillory still stands, although probably unoccupied.

Just past The Lion turn right along a signposted footpath which brings us to Culham Cut, where we turn *left* along the towpath. (Yes, I know; we always walk upstream. But this is not the river, only an artificial cut, dug in 1809. We shall soon be walking upstream along the banks of the real river when we get past Culham Lock, which can be seen ahead). The cut, bypassing a loop in the river and the lovely Sutton Pools which we shall shortly see, was constructed because of the serious obstacle to river traffic posed by a 'flash weir' actually located underneath a mill, a most unusual and awkward arrangement.

Beyond the lock we turn right over the bridge and then over the much older Sutton Bridge beneath which flows the Thames in its original channel. After about a hundred yards, opposite some cottages, a wooden wicket gate on the right allows us to drop down beside the river. Only for a short distance, however, for soon a hedge on the right obliges us to leave the waterside for a while and a stile ahead brings us into a drive. This emerges into a road opposite the Fish Inn at Sutton Courtenay and we note, with relief, that although the footpath we have just walked is not marked on the map as a right of way it is nonetheless signposted here. Turn right for a few yards to

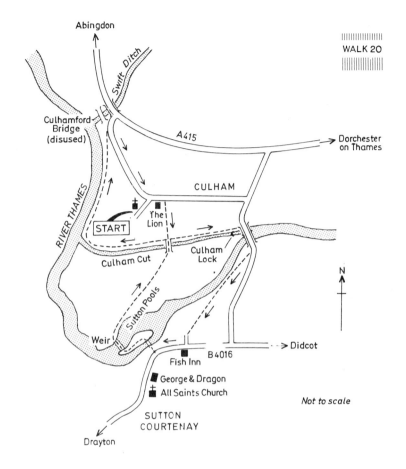

Abingdon

Swift Ditch

Culhamford
Bridge
(disused)

A415

Dorchester
on Thames

RIVER THAMES

CULHAM

START

The
Lion

Culham
Lock

Culham Cut

Sutton Pools

N

Weir

Didcot

B4016

Fish Inn

George & Dragon

All Saints Church

Not to scale

SUTTON
COURTENAY

Drayton

a corner, then go right down a footpath at the side of a long red-brick house.

First, however, you may care to go left to explore the beautiful village. It is full of the most picturesque old houses including, in the twelfth century Norman Hall, one of the two oldest inhabited houses in Berkshire. Just past the George and Dragon is the ancient All Saints Church, parts of which date from Norman times. Three interesting graves are to be found in the churchyard. One is of a Mrs Martha Pye, who died at the age of 117 in 1822; another is of H.H. ('Wait and see') Asquith, who was Prime Minister from 1908 to 1916 and who lived in the village, and the third is of Eric Blair, better known as George Orwell, the author of that horrifying vision of the future, *1984*. Just about now, come to think of it.

We cross a wooden bridge and are again following the original course of the river, and now begins a short walk round a backwater which is, without doubt, one of the most fascinating places on the river. We cross three metal footbridges over weirs and enjoy views across the wide expanses of water known as Sutton Pools. Finally we cross a larger bridge over the main weir, a spectacular sight and an exciting experience when a lot of water is running.

The path bends right and, over a stile, leads over a meadow to another stile where some large stones beneath our feet indicate that this was a causeway across low land liable to flooding. The path climbs gently towards the bridge over Culham Cut, close to a point we passed earlier on, and we turn left along the towpath on the other side. To the right we see the church and Culham Manor again, the latter with its seventeenth century dovecot with accommodation for 4,000 birds.

After about a third of a mile the cut ends and we find ourselves walking once more beside the 'old' river. Just short of a road, which we join beside Tollgate Cottage, the towpath swings left over a rather lovely old wooden footbridge. It is worth diverting a few yards to stand on this bridge. It spans the Swift Ditch which is probably the true main stream of the Thames. However, in the tenth century the monks of Abingdon cut a rival channel through the town and the present navigation was cut a century later. The Swift Ditch was re-opened in 1624 but the present channel was opened again in 1790 when the Swift Ditch once more fell into disuse. The beautiful fifteenth century Culhamford Bridge you see before you, crossing the Swift Ditch, is not in use either.

On reaching the road, turn right. It is a quiet country road with a path on the right-hand side separated from the carriageway by a grassy verge. Didcot power station, ahead, does not actually improve the view yet the giant cooling towers are not without a certain grace. In half a mile we reach the green and, turning right at the pillory, soon reach the church and the car. Perhaps we may meditate, as we cross the green, on those who might profitably be sentenced to a couple of hours in the pillory; vandals and litter-louts, for instance, and farmers who plough up public footpaths and don't reinstate them.

Walk 21   Radley

6½ miles (10.5 km)

OS sheet 164

Much of this walk passes through the landscape enjoyed by Queen Victoria and her beloved Albert from the bedroom window of their honeymoon retreat.

Our starting point is Kennington, almost a suburb of Oxford due south of the city on an unclassified road. A convenient free car park will be found beside the Kennington Health Centre and the Social Club and opposite The Tandem pub.

On leaving the car park we go right, along the road and, opposite St Swithun's Church, turn right into Bagley Wood Road, actually a pleasant country lane. We cross St Swithun's Road to the continuation of Bagley Wood Road but immediately fork right at a Public Footpath sign and climb slightly to a playing field. Our path now runs along the right-hand edge of it to a small wooden gate through which we carry on at the right-hand edge of a field. When the path divides, as it begins to drop down towards a wood, we take the right-hand fork and, still keeping to the right-hand edge of the field, come to a stile and a plank bridge over a stream.

Our way lies along the main path ahead, just within the boundary of the wood, a delightful path indeed. Although it may be a trifle muddy in places, some large stepping stones have been thoughtfully provided in the worst spot. A path joins from the left and another soon after, but we ignore them both and carry on ahead. We ignore, too, a footbridge on our right.

On coming to a small road (Sugworth Lane), we cross to a stile opposite and over the field beyond. The path may not be very plain on the ground but it runs slightly left towards the supporting pole of a power line at the right-hand corner of a small wood. Actually, when we get there we find that the pole stands in the next field but we pass beside it as we cross this second field.

The path then runs beside the right-hand edge of the wood and leads onto the Radley College playing field where — surprisingly — the public right of way lies across the football pitches. It goes in a slightly leftward direction, but if a game is in progress the prudent pedestrian will doubtless make his way round the edge of the field. The right of way then passes to the left of a running track and, when the track

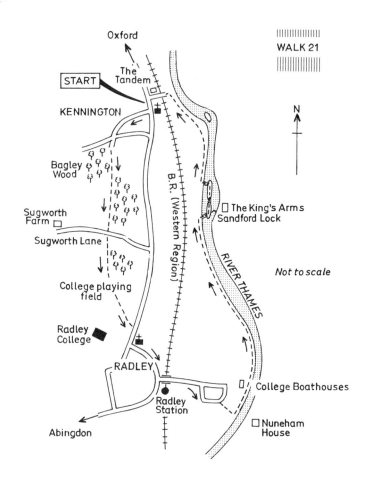

Oxford

The Tandem

START

KENNINGTON

Bagley Wood

Sugworth Farm

Sugworth Lane

B.R. (Western Region)

The King's Arms
Sandford Lock

RIVER THAMES

Not to scale

N

College playing field

Radley College

RADLEY

Radley Station

College Boathouses

Abingdon

Nuneham House

curves round right, drops towards a wooden gate beside an iron one. Our route is then left along a grassy path to a road, reached through a kissing gate at a footpath sign.

Turn right along the road and come to St James the Great church on the left. The church must be visited for it is rich in treasures. There is some gorgeous Tudor stained glass (and some even older) the most notable being in the west window where Henry VII is depicted in hunting gear. The charming house which is now the vicarage served him as a hunting lodge. The ornate woodwork, acquired by the church in 1653 and which stands behind the pulpit, was formerly part of the Speaker's chair in the House of Commons. The seventeenth century misericordes in the choir came from Germany and are a reminder that the religious order called the Community of the

Resurrection (now at Mirfield in West Yorkshire) was founded here in Radley by a former vicar, Charles Gore, later Bishop Gore.

Turn left into Church Road, go left over the railway and then, after passing the entrance to a gravel pit, turn right at a white house. The lane soon bends left and, when it begins to bend left again, fork right past a house numbered 87. A tiny stone in the grass says 'Public Footpath to River Thames' but this could easily be missed. The track bends, runs across the field roughly in the direction of a boathouse, and meets the towpath, where we turn left.

Across the water is Nuneham House. With a Royal Standard flying directly over their bedroom, Victoria and Albert spent their honeymoon here. Incidentally, when the house was built by the first Earl of Harcourt in the eighteenth century he not only demolished the old manor house but an entire village as well, shifting the inhabitants to a new location on the Dorchester road. This improved his view.

Soon we pass the Radley College boathouses. Now put this book away and simply enjoy the sights and sounds of the river until you reach Sandford Lock with Sandford Mill beside it.

A concrete bridge crosses the water to the lock and a permissive path over the lock and a footbridge will take you, if you wish, to the King's Arms where a brass plate fixed half-way up the counter in one of the bars marks the level the flood water reached one appalling March day in 1947. A visit to the pub is a diversion, however. Our route, immediately after we have crossed the concrete bridge, passes to the left of the lock and along the towpath, crossing two footbridges over weir streams.

Across a metal footbridge, further along, we turn right. Then, beyond a gate after about 100 yards, our path goes slightly left over a somewhat marshy meadow, bypassing a loop of the river. Here it was that in the twelfth century Matilda, daughter of Henry I, wife of the Holy Roman Emperor Henry V and rightful Queen of England, escaped the clutches of the usurping Stephen by crossing the frozen Thames after sliding down a rope from Oxford Castle.

To the left you will see a metal footbridge which will take you over the railway. On the other side of the line a road brings us up beside The Tandem. The car park is on the opposite side of the main road.

Walk 22   Oxford

5¾ miles (9.5 km)

OS sheet 164

I call this the 'Alice in Wonderland' walk. This is because we shall be walking beside the stretch of the Thames between Oxford and Godstow on which it is believed that, on 4 July 1862, Lewis Carroll rowed little Alice Liddell and began to weave his immortal story around her.

It is an interesting and easy walk, on good paths throughout and all on much the same level. Also, it is by the waterside nearly all the way, for we go out along the river Thames and back along the Oxford Canal.

The only difficulty likely to be encountered will be before you start, in trying to find somewhere to park. The starting point of our ramble is Osney Bridge over the Thames on the Botley Road (A420), west of Oxford railway station. Just west of the bridge is a small bridge with 'Osney Town' on it and immediately left over this bridge is North Street where there is 24-hour parking for a few cars. North Street leads to East Street beside the river, where there is parking limited to three hours (I found a place here.) If all fails, there will certainly be space in Ferry Hinksey Road (signposted 'Osney Mead Industrial Estate') at traffic lights a little further west along Botley Road, but this will add ten minutes or so to your walking time.

The Thames takes several channels through Oxford. In times past numerous cuts were constructed to serve water mills. What seems today to be the main channel, and the one we are about to follow, was probably dug by the monks of Osney Abbey to work the wheel of their mill.

Our ramble starts at the north-east corner of the bridge over the Thames where a little slope runs down to the towpath. The first two or three hundred yards of towpath are not very attractive but the houses are soon left behind. We cross a graceful iron footbridge over the entrance to the cut linking the river to the canal and astonishingly — as if a curtain had been lifted — we are immediately in open country and there is water on either side.

After some distance we pass through a gate and over a bridge, ignoring a bridge on the right which leads to the Medley Boat Station. Soon the towpath ends and we cross the river by a footbridge and

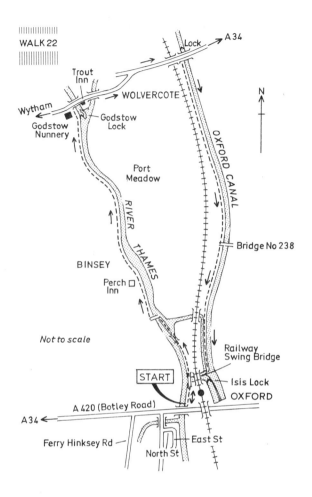

resume our previous direction on the other bank. The river broadens at this point and the great Port Meadow comes into view, 439 acres of common land held by the freepersons of Oxford since before the time of Edward the Confessor.

Keep beside the water and pass through a couple of gates when you will see, to the left, the tiny group of cottages at Binsey. Pass (or not pass, as the case may be) a stile on the left inviting a diversion to the Perch Inn at Binsey; the thatched inn is much closer to the river than the cottages we observed just now.

Continue along the towpath and come, eventually, to Godstow Lock. Turn round here for a glance at Oxford's distant 'dreaming spires'. Then we come to the ruins of Godstow Nunnery, founded in

1133 and inhabited at first by the widows and unmarried female relatives of Norman kings and noblemen.

The towpath meets the road at the narrow double-arched Godstow bridge. Cross the bridge carefully and come to the delightful old Trout Inn, formerly the guest house of the nunnery, with its terrace patrolled by a peacock, overlooking the weir. Make your way along Godstow Road and come to a bridge over a mill stream. Just on the other side of the bridge is a touching memorial to two officers of the Royal Flying Corps who were killed when their monoplane crashed 100 yards from this spot on 10 September 1912; touching, but interesting, with its pictorial representation of the flimsy aircraft.

We follow the road round to the left and then right, through Wolvercote, then left and right behind a children's play area. Further along the road ahead (it is still called Godstow Road) we pass beside Wolvercote Common. Make sure you cross the road to its left-hand side before you reach the railway bridge; you will see why when you get there.

Immediately beyond the railway bridge drop down a steep path on the left to the canal towpath. There is a lock here, but diminutive compared with the Thames locks we have seen. Turn right.

The Oxford Canal is one of the oldest. It was authorised in 1769 and the first canal boat reached Oxford on 2 January 1790. Nuffield College now stands on the site of the former canal basin and wharf in Oxford. Bridge No 238 will turn out, when you reach it, to be of an interesting type common on the canals — a lifting bridge. Heavy as they are, they are usually easy to operate, being so nicely balanced.

Eventually, after passing a weir and a turning basin, we come to the elegant bridge No 243 by Isis Lock. Do not cross this bridge, however, but go right over a much less elegant one which takes us onto the towpath beside one of the connecting cuts between canal and river. You will notice a railway swing bridge. Opening and closing it is a laborious task and, over the years, this swing bridge has been cursed by boatmen and railwaymen alike.

All but the shortest of us will have to stoop to pass beneath the next bridge and then we find ourselves beside the Thames again. Turn left at the footbridge and soon we are back where we started, at Osney Bridge. This area seems to be rich in awkward or low bridges, for Osney Bridge (you will not be surprised to learn when you look at it from the towpath) has the lowest headroom of any on the river.

Walk 23   Wytham

5¼ miles (8.5 km)

OS sheet 164

This easy walk starts and finishes in the tiny village of Wytham, which lies on a minor road that leaves the Oxford Ring Road (A34) about a mile north of the intersection with the A420. Alternatively, it can be approached by a minor road from Wolvercote which passes underneath the A34.

With its mellow stones and thatched buildings Wytham could almost be in the Cotswolds. There is an inn called the White Hart and several odd corners in which you may park discreetly.

Our expedition starts unfortunately, but unavoidably, with ten minutes of road walking on a road out of Wytham signposted 'Godstow and Wolvercote'. Yet not much traffic will be met upon it and you will pass an interesting ancient monument on your right just before reaching the river at Godstow bridge. This is the ruined Godstow Nunnery, an aristocratic establishment founded in 1133 and generously supported by the Norman kings and noblemen as a suitable retreat for their widows and unmarried womenfolk. You may care to know, if you didn't visit the White Hart before you started and now wish you had, that there is a fine old inn called The Trout just over the bridge with a delightful garden, patrolled by a peacock and overlooking the weir stream. The bridge is picturesque but horribly narrow; it is also, I believe, tricky for boats to navigate.

However, if you do not cross the bridge, turn left onto the towpath by a sign saying 'Eynsham 4 miles'. The towpath soon passes beneath the A34. At a point, shortly reached, where the river makes a right-angle bend to the right, many walkers appear to take a short cut over the meadow towards King's Lock (the weir machinery of which can be seen ahead), thereby avoiding two loops in the river.

Carry on past the lock, above which is Duke's Cut which joins the Oxford Canal. Cross a footbridge over the weir on the Seacourt Stream — a little river we passed over earlier on our way out of Wytham — and immediately another short cut, avoiding a loop in the river, may tempt you. From now onwards there is not always a good path and much of the way is over grass. But keep near the water's edge and you can't go wrong.

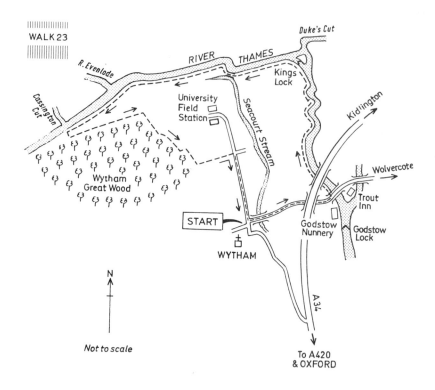

Duke's Cut

RIVER THAMES

R. Evenlode

Kings Lock

Cassington Cut

University Field Station

Seacourt Stream

Kidlington

Wolvercote

Wytham Great Wood

Trout Inn

START

Godstow Nunnery

Godstow Lock

WYTHAM

N

A34

Not to scale

To A420 & OXFORD

On the other side of the river we pass the entry of the river Evenlode and, a little later, an old canal, the disused Cassington Cut on which barges used to reach Cassington mill. Here we leave the riverside. Exactly opposite the Cassington Cut a gate and stile are met. Instead of crossing the stile, turn sharply left and follow round the right-hand edge of the field, with a barbed wire fence and the dense Wytham Great Wood on your right. For a short distance you will find yourself walking parallel with the towpath on which you have come.

It is not much of a path we are now upon, but the going is quite easy and if you keep close to the fence all will be well. Press on all the way to the end of this side of the wood. When, towards the end, the trees begin to give way to bushes, still carry on as near the fence as you can, although the path for the next 180 yards is not easy to discern on the ground.

Then you will see, over a stile, a long, straight cart-track on the right going towards a distant part of the wood. Follow this track, which gently rises. When the wood is reached, the track bears slightly left but when, after 60 yards, it sweeps away to the left over the field, continue on the path ahead, keeping close to the fence and the trees.

You come to a ditch and the path does a right-angle turn to the left. Soon, a small railway-sleeper bridge takes you over the ditch to a stile, and having crossed this, cross another stile just ahead. Proceed up the right-hand edge of the field to yet another stile. Beyond this a sleeper-bridge crosses another ditch and the path goes on at the right-hand edge of another field.

At the end of this field the path bears slightly left, another sleeper-bridge crosses another ditch and you pass through the hedge onto a wide track. Turn left and follow this all the way to a lane, and turn right for the short distance back into Wytham.

Walk 24   Northmoor

5½ or 3 miles (9 or 5 km)

OS sheet 164

A 'figure of eight' walk in which the top or the bottom circle alone obviously provides a shorter walk for anyone wishing to undertake something less than the complete route. I recommend the upper circle because this includes a reach of the Thames.

Take the B4449 road north-east from the A415 about half-way between Abingdon and Witney. At a sharp left-hand turn on this B road, a minor road leads to Northmoor, our starting point, where you can park near the twelfth century church of St Denys.

Go back a short distance on the road on which you came and turn left down Moreton Lane. Sixty-five yards after crossing a tiny bridge, a cart track on the left leads 25 yards to an iron field gate. Beyond this, follow the invisible path along the right-hand edge of the field until you come to a field gate on the right. Go through it, and then through (or over) a 'barbed wire gate' opposite, but don't turn left. Then make your way round the right-hand edge of the field beneath the power lines — it is still hard to see the path — and come to a rough stile in the corner of the field. Over the stile a narrow plank bridge has to be crossed, a small ditch negotiated and a bank scrambled up (a bit of an adventure all this!). In effect, jink right, then left.

The path then goes on along the left-hand edge of a field to a much more substantial footbridge in its corner and a stile. The path then takes you at the left-hand edge of the field to another stile. Maintain your direction, past a short length of hedge on the left, and across the middle of a large field and come out, over a small stream and a stile, into a field. Make towards a large, curved footbridge you can now see, half-right. This isolated bridge is on the site of Hart's Weir, long dismantled. During the years that the weir existed a right of way across it — dangerous as that undoubtedly was — became established. When the weir was removed the right of way was maintained; hence the present footbridge.

For the shorter walk, you must not cross the bridge but turn right. Skip the next two paragraphs.

The more energetic of us, however, cross the bridge and on the other side of the river Thames, follow the path over a small concrete footbridge. Jinking right, then left, follow a grassy route to a gap

76

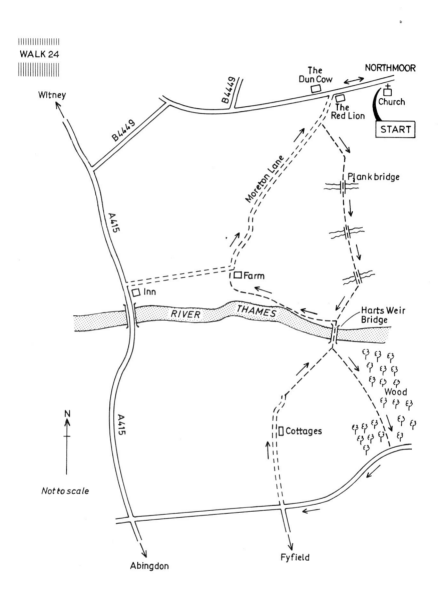

WALK 24

Witney

B4449

B4449

A415

NORTHMOOR

The Dun Cow

The Red Lion

Church

START

Moreton Lane

Plank bridge

Farm

Inn

RIVER   THAMES

Harts Weir Bridge

Wood

N

A415

Cottages

Not to scale

Abingdon

Fyfield

77

where the path is composed of large concrete lumps. (As you will observe, all the paths on this side of the river are better and more visible than those on the other side.) Now take a grassy path bearing slightly left towards an electricity pylon and then running along the left-hand edge of the field with a wood on its left. Ignore a 'Bridleway' sign on an entry into the wood. Come to a stile, and carry on along the left edge of the next field to a swing gate leading into the wood, through which the path continues with a barbed wire fence on your left. You come out at a stile, and turn right along the road for half a mile or so until you reach a road going left to Fyfield and Tubney.

Almost opposite is a rough road on the *right*, which you take. After you pass a couple of cottages and a wide view opens up, the rough road degenerates to a cart track. It goes right after a metal gate, soon becoming a grassy track and bending left. At the end of a fence to the right, it heads slightly right across a field and eventually comes to the gap, with the concrete lumps underfoot where you have been before. This is the 'waist' of our figure of eight. You will remember the path to Hart's Weir Bridge over the Thames, on the other side of which turn left.

Those on the shorter walk re-join us here to make our way along the towpath — not that you can actually see any path — for a few yards to a stile. Cross it carefully for the river bank is eroded here. You come after some distance to a gate across the path, which may have to be climbed. Beyond it, the river bank is contained by a short length of concrete walling and, at the end of it, you reach a metal gate. Here we must leave the river.

Strike slightly away from the waterside and, with some small trees on your right at first, curve round, rightwards, to pass to the left of some farm buildings and come to a lane. Go right, but because the lane bends sharply left, you resume your previous direction. This is a pleasant, leafy lane and towards the end you will realise that it is, in fact, Moreton Lane on which you set out earlier in the day. And as you approach Northmoor, where your car awaits, you will see The Dun Cow on your left and The Red Lion on your right.

4¼ miles (7 km)

OS sheet 164

I found a lot of mud on this walk and vegetation encroaches on the towpath. So let us say this walk is best undertaken in early spring before the nettles and brambles have sprung up, and after a dry period.

The starting place is the village of Longworth, which may be reached along any one of several minor roads running north from the A420 about nine miles south-west of Oxford. Park discreetly near the eastern end of the village (Rodney Place) or perhaps in the side road named Bow Bank and signposted 'Longworth School'.

Start walking from the eastern end of the village where, at Rodney Place, the road swings right in the direction of the main road, and turn left along a private road signposted as a public footpath. When the tarmac ends carry on along the track ahead until you reach a farm where the track turns sharply left. Here, we jink right to pass the farm buildings along a grassy path, soon coming to a signposted bridleway, where we turn left.

The way is metalled until the farm is passed, then we fork right along a sandy lane. Just past a thatched byre on the left we come to a junction of three bridleways and a sign ahead saying 'Private, No Right of Way'. Here we turn right through a 6-bar tubular metal gate (our way being indicated by one of the signs) and proceed along the left-hand edge of a field towards another gate. Through this, our way continues as before near the left-hand edge of a field until, at the top of it, a wooden gate leads into the A415 road, in which we turn left.

But not for long. In two or three hundred yards we reach the river Thames at Newbridge. The narrow bridge, which is one of the oldest on the river, was fought over in a Civil War battle in 1644. On this side is The Maybush and on the other side The Rose Revived.

We gain access to the towpath along a path at the left-hand side of The Maybush. The first part of our riverside walk lies through wide meadows, but after a while we reach a stretch where trees and bushes have grown up beside the water. The path near the water's edge may be somewhat overgrown, but I found it passable though muddy in places.

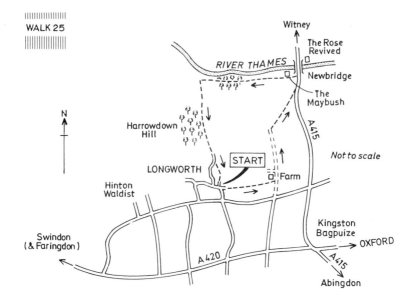

After a time we go through a grey-painted gate, and a few hundred yards beyond this we cross a footbridge with a gate at either end. Now be a little careful. We leave the riverside here and bear left towards a makeshift gate of barbed wire in the barbed wire fence. This 'gate' gives access to a path which crosses a tiny hump-back bridge and climbs to a field. The path runs at the right-hand edge of the field, slowly climbing towards tree-clad Harrowdown Hill, and at the top of the field a gate brings us to a track, which we cross. Our way continues ahead through another gate opposite and along a more or less straight — but muddy — path running up and over the hill.

The path comes out into a lane by the entrance to a house called Tuck's Mead. We turn left in the lane and bear right with it. At white-painted Glebe Cottage we cross its drive to a stile by a footpath sign. Over the stile, we make our way along the right-hand edge of a field. At the top of it the path bends right round the side of a playing field, and comes to a stile leading into Bow Bank, one of the roads in which you may have parked your car.

80

Walk 26   Tadpole Bridge

6¾ miles (11 km)

OS sheet 164

Definitely among the book's Top Ten walks, this is a delightful ramble through marvellously peaceful and remote countryside and along a most attractive reach of the Thames. Except for the landlord and a couple of customers in the pub (conveniently located around the mid-point of the walk) I hardly met a soul all day.

The starting point is miles from anywhere, too. Running north from the A420 about half-way between Oxford and Swindon is a minor road signposted 'Littleworth and Thrupp'. Drive carefully on the twisting road through Littleworth, a pleasant village with a disappointing church (which, nevertheless, will interest students of the Tractarian Movement) and drive down a long and straight, but narrow, road. After nearly a mile and a half it bends very sharply left. There is room on the grass verge, either just before or just round the bend, to park off the road. This is our starting point.

A hundred yards *short* of the bend we turn into a lane signposted 'Bridleway'. There is a thick hedge on either side of the lane but through the gaps in it we glimpse pleasant views of a pastoral landscape. We pass a farm and go through a tumbledown gate across our way, beyond which the lane (now a track) bends sharply right to Pucketty Farm. We do not go round with the track, however, but go straight ahead on a cart track.

After negotiating an iron field gate across the track, pause for a moment. The right of way now diverges slightly leftwards from the track to bypass the extensive farm buildings ahead, although the path we must follow is, for the most part, invisible on the ground. It runs behind the nearby pair of red-brick cottages. Cross the grass and come to a wooden footbridge followed by a makeshift stile. Beyond this, the path runs across the field, passing approximately 100 yards to the left of the red-brick farm buildings, through a wire fence and over another wooden footbridge. (It's a bit muddy around here.) The path then crosses the next field, heading *very* slightly to the right of a farmhouse ahead, and emerges through a 6-bar tubular metal gate back onto the track (or perhaps one should say 'lane' again now) at a bend. Carry on along the lane (not the track running towards the farm) to pass the farm on your left.

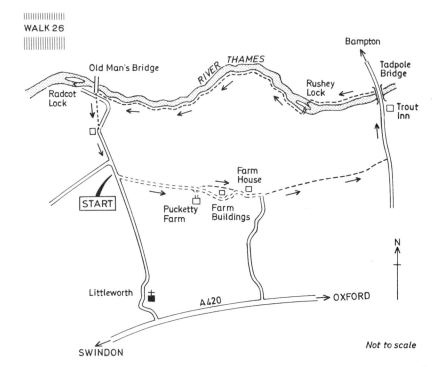

At a corner, where the lane bends sharply right, bear slightly left at a 'Public Bridleway' sign, past a group of delightful cottages and through a wooden field gate. Despite the sign, the bridleway is not much to look at on the ground but it goes along the left-hand edge of the field. Ignore a small stile you may notice on the left.

The view to the right gets more and more attractive. Our path jinks right, then left, and follows the left-hand edge of another field at the end of which we come to a crossing track. We go ahead, jinking slightly right, to pass along the left-hand edge of yet another field. Then, beyond an iron gate, the path goes *through* the field, heading at first more or less directly towards a large house ahead. But when the next field is reached the path runs at the right-hand edge of it and comes to a gate leading into a road.

Turn left for half a mile to Tadpole Bridge. I'm sorry about this unavoidable bit of road walking but it's a fairly quiet and quite picturesque country road. And when we come to the bridge we are rewarded, for beside it stands the Trout Inn, a welcome sight maybe.

Cross the fine old bridge (nearly 200 years old) and go down left onto the towpath, the Water Authority road as far as Rushey Lock. The river banks are high above the water here and colourful with a rich variety of wild flowers. We come to the lock through a gate on the left. There is a permissive way over the lock gates and, by passing to the left of the lock-keeper's cottage, to the weir. This weir, which is one of the few that still retain the paddle construction of weirs of an earlier age, will fascinate any reader who has an interest in inland navigation. In his mind's eye he will soon gain a picture of how a 'flash' weir operated before pound locks were introduced.

Over the weir we turn right along the towpath, through a gate and shortly across a footbridge over a stream. No matter where one looks along the next stretch there is not a glimpse of human habitation.

From here to Radcot Lock, along what I think is one of the most delightful reaches of the river, the Thames twists and turns and one ought (I suppose) to resist the temptation to take short cuts. The well-trodden path, however, has no such misgivings. I shall not attempt to describe all the contortions of the path over the next mile or so; it is not always plain on the ground and somewhat overgrown anyway. If you keep the river *somewhere* to your right you won't get lost.

We pass what looks like two ancient burial mounds. They are not shown as such on the 1:50,000 Ordnance Survey map although I note a nearby stream is called Burroway Brook. Just beyond, we cross a footbridge over a tributary stream.

Shortly, you will notice a small bridge with wooden railings to your left, which carries the little road from Radcot Lock to more populous parts. Ahead and slightly to the right is a large footbridge crossing the river. This is called Old Man's Bridge and we make towards it, but do not cross it.

If you wish to make the short diversion to Radcot Lock carry on along the towpath and then come back to this point.

Turn your back squarely to Old Man's Bridge and walk ahead near the right-hand edge of the meadow, a hedge on your right, along a path that is at first not very visible. Pass through a row of trees and come eventually to a stile, which cross. (The little road from the lock converges on this point.) Turn left along the lane, which soon bends right and then goes straight ahead to join the road at the bend, near your starting point.

Walk 27   Lechlade

5½ or 4 miles (9 or 6.5 km)

OS sheet 163

This is not only a pleasant ramble in the countryside around one of the most attractive Thames-side towns but it also marks a significant stage in our series of walks. For Lechlade is the highest point to which the Thames was navigable by commercial vessels and so, a mile above the town, the towpath ends. Although we shall find riverside paths to follow on our subsequent rambles we shall no longer have a towpath to tread.

Our starting point is the village of Buscot, which lies to the north of the A417 a couple of miles on the Faringdon side of Lechlade. Through the village, you will find on the right-hand side the (free) Buscot Weir car park. Park here.

On leaving the car park, turn right along the lane through part of the 4,000 acres the National Trust owns around these parts. Across a small bridge immediately turn right along a signposted footpath to the lock and weir. This path leads over a new footbridge above a weir, over the upper lock gates (across which there is a permissive way) and then over a bridge above a newly-constructed weir. Pass through a wooden gate and turn left along the towpath, with wide meadows ahead.

When the river makes a deep loop you will probably find yourself following the short cut that ramblers' feet have trodden out to bypass it. Soon, however, we must leave the riverside for a while, so where the river bends slightly left, we pass through a wicket gate beside a metal farm gate. A very pleasant track brings us to a little road in which we turn left. Take your bearings here for we pass this way again later.

At a T-junction, turn left past the Trout Inn and over St John's Bridge; there has been a bridge here for seven hundred years. A sloping path on the right drops down to St John's Lock, the highest lock on the river. Beside the lock reclines the bearded figure of Father Thames, a statue commissioned in 1854 for the Crystal Palace and presented to the Thames Conservators in 1958. At first they stationed it at the river's source at Thames Head but prudently translated it to this more vandal-free location in 1974.

Once past the lock, we are on the towpath again and make our way towards Lechlade's Halfpenny Bridge, so named because that was the sum exacted as a toll from pedestrians until 1839. We pass through

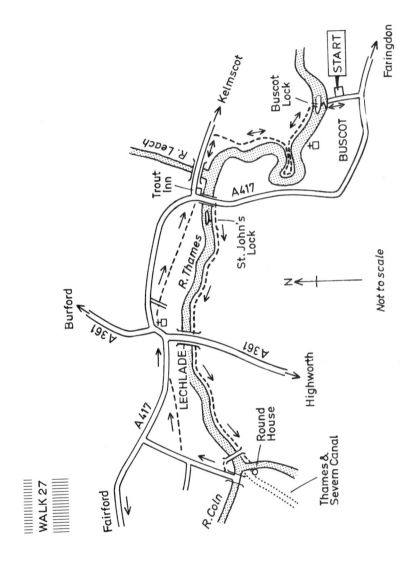

WALK 27

START

Faringdon

Buscot Lock

Kelmscot

R. Leach

BUSCOT

Trout Inn

A417

St. John's Lock

R. Thames

N

Not to scale

Burford

A361

A361

Highworth

LECHLADE

A417

Fairford

Round House

R.Coln

Thames & Severn Canal

a tunnel beneath the bridge, and those wishing to undertake the shorter walk now turn left, up the steps and over the bridge into the town, rejoining the rest of us two paragraphs ahead. We will rendezvous by the church.

The more energetic of us continue along the towpath for a mile through parklike countryside to a sturdy footbridge spanning the river. Don't cross it, however, until you have walked along the last few yards of the towpath to the Round House standing sentinel at the entrance to the Thames and Severn Canal. Opened in 1789, it linked our two greatest rivers. But Fortune never smiled on this union between Tamesis and the fair Sabrina and the canal fell into disuse at the end of the last century.

Retracing our steps to the footbridge, we cross it and along a path beside the river Coln (which joins the Thames just here), come to a stile leading into a drive. We turn right and, on reaching a lane, turn right again. Then, where the lane almost immediately bends left, we go ahead over a stile. The path that now lies before us crosses more stiles than I have ever encountered in such a short distance! Maintain your direction across fields in a slightly leftward direction over stile after stile after stile until the path reaches a stile leading into a path between houses. A final stile—a stone one, for a change— gives onto a road. Turn right for the few yards into the centre of Lechlade.

At the north side of the church runs Shelley's Path, so called because it was here, in 1815, that Percy Bysshe composed his *A Summer Evening Churchyard, Lechlade*. At the end of the churchyard we cross Wharf Lane and continue on the path opposite. This is a very ancient path which linked the church with St John's Priory, dissolved even before the Reformation. We come out on the road close to the Trout Inn and cross to the Kelmscot road opposite and for the rest of the way we find ourselves retracing the route we took on our outward journey.

But things always look different when viewed from another direction. Carry on along the road to the gate on the right through which we came earlier and turn through it again. On reaching the river we follow it till we come to the wooden gate which gives access to the Buscot Lock area. Then, after crossing over the bridges and the lock, we can make our way up the lane to the car park.

Walk 28   Cricklade

4¾ miles (7.5 km)
OS sheet 163

Cricklade is an important point in the scheme of this book for, just as Lechlade marks the highest point to which commercial craft could navigate the Thames, so Cricklade is just about the highest point that can be reached by the smallest pleasure craft. The river hereabouts is little more than a large stream.

You may find a few muddy patches on the walk. Yet it is not a difficult one and there are points of unusual interest, especially for the canal enthusiast.

The starting point is the village of Latton, which is on the A419(T) Swindon to Cirencester road about five miles south of the latter and about a mile north of Cricklade. A 'Latton' sign appears beside the A419 at either end of the village but the main part of it, and the church, lie along a presently unsignposted road running north-east from the main road. Take this minor road and park near the church.

Start walking along the lane at the south side of the church and come, at the end of the made-up section, to a double footpath sign. Do not take the clear, fenced path to the left but the invisible one to the right. Pass through a large wooden gate and then through another, half-right, ahead. The path, or rather the line of the path, runs across the field towards a wooden gate that can be seen in the hedge on the far side.

The gate has a small gate beside it and, through this, continue near the right-hand edge of a field to a stile. We cross the stile and continue our direction along the right-hand edge of the next field to another stile. Beyond this the path carries on again at the right-hand edge of another field until, at the end of it, we cross a double stile and come out into a narrow road.

A footpath sign opposite points to Eisey (it is 'Eysey' on the map) and Calcott and we follow the path—actually a cart track—on the right-hand side of a stream. (The Ordnance map, curiously, shows the right of way as being on the other bank, but there is no path over there and the signpost certainly indicates the path we are following.) After passing a tubular metal gate the way becomes indistinct but keep about the same distance from the stream as before. On coming to a footbridge reached over an easy-to-climb fence, cross the stream

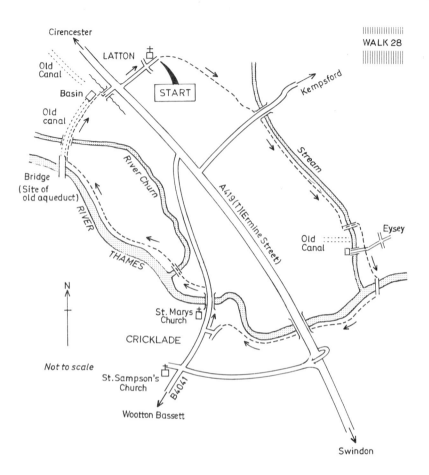

and turn right along its bank. Then, just short of a cottage, scramble up through the bushes (it's a bit overgrown here) to a triple footpath sign by a footbridge.

There was clearly an aqueduct here in former times which carried the Thames and Severn Canal over the stream, and the sign pointing to 'Ermine Street' points along the canal's overgrown towpath. We go the other way, however, towards 'Calcott and Cricklade'. The path leads over a stile, across a lane in front of the cottage and continues opposite along the left bank of the stream. Soon we reach a stile beyond which it is easy to walk. We make towards a metal footbridge to be seen slightly to the left ahead and find that we have at last reached the Thames.

On the other side of the river, turn right beside it. Now the noise of traffic on the busy A419 begins to intrude on the peaceful scene as we pass through a small wooden gate and then, shortly, climb a stile. Cross a concrete footbridge over a tributary stream and continue with the Thames on the right. Just before reaching the main road we climb another stile and go beneath the road, with the river. We cross another stile, then a footbridge over another stream, then another stile and make our way along a rather muddy track towards Cricklade, still with the Thames on our right.

A stile by a gate (probably open) takes us out of the field. Now, be careful. Don't go ahead by a concrete causeway but go along the right-hand edge of the small field to a stile in the corner and cross it into a rough lane. Turn left, and then right into Abingdon Court Lane. This leads into Cricklade's main street. Turn right, unless you wish to explore this attractive town which has a history going back to Roman times. It is said to have been a seat of learning in the seventh century, five hundred years before Oxford University was founded.

Our walk continues down the main street, past the redundant St Mary's Church, bearing left with the road and crossing a bridge over the Thames. Ignore a footpath sign·just before the bridge indicating 'West Mill Lane' but continue along the road a little further to another sign, similarly worded, and turn left here and cross a stile. The path then goes half-right across the field to a stile in the corner where we reach the riverside again, and cross a footbridge over the river Churn where it flows into the Thames. Rising at Seven Springs, near Cheltenham, this unimpressive little river is the highest source of Thames water.

Now we are in Cricklade's North Meadow, a nature reserve. After a while a thick hedge obliges us to leave the river bank briefly, but soon another footbridge brings us back, although it takes us temporarily out of the nature reserve. Cross the field towards the river but do not cross a bridge over it; instead turn right along the bank. Through a wooden gate we carry on along the path by the riverside and, at a gate in the hedge, re-enter the North Meadow nature reserve.

Next we come to a farm bridge on the site of a former aqueduct. You can still find some remains of this old aqueduct which carried the North Wilts Canal over the river.

We climb up to, and over, a stile by the bridge but do not cross the bridge. Instead, we turn right along the rough path ahead and through the trees — the old canal towpath. The canal appears as an indentation on the left. It is hard to believe that this was quite an important little waterway in its time. Opened in 1819, it ran from a basin (which we shall shortly see) at Latton on the Thames and Severn Canal, to join the Wilts and Berks Canal near Swindon. By allowing traffic bound for London (principally coal) to reach the Thames at Abingdon instead of Lechlade, the shallower and longer navigation of the upper reaches of the river was avoided.

A large wooden footbridge soon takes us over the river Churn and to a stile. Beyond this, despite the fairly clear path ahead (which common usage seems to favour) the right of way, according to the map, switches to the other side of the canal. Since there is no water in it, this presents no problem. Yet when the path on the other side becomes impassable a little further along it seems to cross back again! We negotiate two more stiles and come, past the remains of a lock, to Latton Basin, now sadly derelict though once probably a scene of bustling activity.

On reaching water ahead — a stream, not the old Thames and Severn Canal, of which all trace seems to have vanished around here — turn right, squeeze past a pair of iron gates and turn left over a bridge. A rough lane leads from here to the main road (A419), coming out by a sign indicating 'The Basin'.

Turn right for a few yards then cross the road and turn left into Latton village where you left your car.

Walk 29   Somerford Keynes

4¼ miles (7 km)

OS sheet 163

This walk starts and finishes in Somerford Keynes, an attractive
Cotswold village clustering around its church and manor house. It is
not a difficult walk, being all on much the same level, though perhaps
it is not ideal for beginners. There is a ditch to be jumped, for
instance, and barbed wire to negotiate. Yet it goes through some very
pleasant countryside which more than compensates for the fact that
the Thames is not an impressive sight around here. In fact, it comes
as a surprise to find the river (in an artificial channel, actually) so
narrow and sluggish. Yet one reads that once upon a time the highest
water mill on the Thames was at Ewen, which we visit today.

Somerford Keynes is the meeting point of several unclassified roads.
Without going into elaborate detail its position can best be described
as being about four miles due south of Cirencester, or about
2½ miles south-east of Kemble, or about five miles west (actually
very slightly north-west) of Cricklade.

Park discreetly in the village, perhaps on the grassy verge of the
'No Through Road' which turns off towards the church by the old
school, now an antique shop.

Immediately beyond the old school is a signposted public footpath.
This is where our walk begins. Not very plainly on the ground, the
path runs half-left across the field towards a stone-built cottage and to
a field gate behind it which becomes visible as you approach. It then
runs half-right across another field to a pair of double wooden gates.

A grassy track leads through these gates and where it bears slightly
to the right in the middle of the field the path goes ahead, towards the
distant buildings of Upper Mill Farm.

Come to a small wooden gate in the hedge just to the right of a
solitary oak tree. Since the gate doesn't open, it has to be treated as
a stile, and climbed. The path then goes along the left-hand edge of a
field towards the farm and leads through a gate into the farm
approach road. Turn right briefly, then left beside the farm buildings
and resume your former direction.

Soon, at a point below a huge barn, a wide gap in the hedge (the
gate, at the time of writing, is collapsed) leads to the riverside. Do
not cross the river by the small concrete bridge on your left.

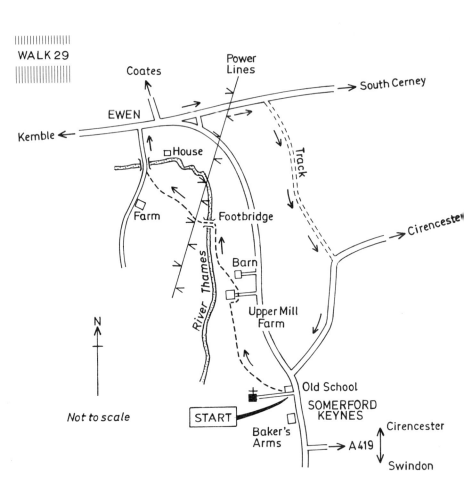

WALK 29

Coates

Power Lines

South Cerney

EWEN

Kemble ←

□ House

Track

Cirencester

Farm

Footbridge

Barn

River Thames

Upper Mill Farm

N

Not to scale

Old School

START

SOMERFORD KEYNES

Baker's Arms

A 419

Cirencester

Swindon

Follow the path beside the river, recovering (if you can) from your surprise at its unimpressive aspect along here, being full of rushes and reeds and other greenery. In point of fact, this is an artificial cut, dug long ago to improve the flow of water through countryside notoriously prone to flooding. About a quarter of a mile along we come to a footbridge. Fortunately, it seems stronger than it looks. Upon arriving safely on the other side of the river and over a stile, go half-right across the field to a rough crossing place over what is now a ditch but which is actually, I fancy, the original course of the Thames. Look around for the easiest place to jump it. Then go up a small field beyond towards a gate at the top, almost beneath some electric power lines. Now go along the top edge of the field, a hedge on your left, for a few yards to a wide gap exactly beneath the power lines; probably there was once a stile here.

The path, invisible on the ground, now goes half-right across the field. Aim towards a point about 100 yards to the right of farm buildings ahead. Through a gate, the way goes ahead towards a stile of sorts at a footpath sign lying roughly mid-way between the farm on the left and a rather lovely old house on the right. The stile leads directly to an ancient stone bridge over the Thames.

Cross the bridge and make your way the short distance up the lane to the hamlet of Ewen (Old English for 'source of a river') and turn right at the T-junction. Ignore the turning for Coates and, admiring the curious porch made of privet on a house we shortly pass, bend left with the road when a 'No Entry' lane comes in ahead. Pass the Wild Duck inn, ignoring the minor road to the left of it, and go beneath our old friends the power lines again. Then, after about another quarter of a mile, turn right along a rough lane, or track, and carry on along it until you reach a quiet country road, in which turn right to Somerford Keynes. The old school is one of the first buildings you come to in the village and your car is nearby. Not far down the road, as you may have discovered before you set off, is a very friendly inn, the Baker's Arms.

Walk 30   The Source

3¼ miles (5.25 km)

OS sheet 163

One approaches the source of the Thames with mixed feelings.
There is the satisfaction of having at last reached journey's end, but
there is also the nagging doubt as to whether this really *is* the source.
The truth is that the Thames is served by more than one spring.
Seven Springs, three miles from Cheltenham, is perhaps the strongest
rival contender and a stone tablet stands there inscribed *Hic Tuus
O Tamisine Pater Septemgeminus Fons* which translated
means 'Here, O Father Thames, is your sevenfold fount'. Yet
although the Seven Springs may be the highest source of Thames
water, they feed the river Churn, which is but a tributary of the
Thames. (We crossed it on Walk 28.) Thames Head in Trewbury
Mead, which we shall visit today, is considered by most authorities,
ancient and modern, to be the river's true source. But it is rare indeed
to see a drop of water rising there!

Our walk starts from a point on the A429 about half a mile from
Kemble in the Cirencester direction. Just past a farm there is a small,
rough, unsigned layby on each side of the road and a footpath sign on
each side, too. Park here. These laybys are actually on the bridge
which carries the road over the often dry bed of the river Thames; it is
the final road bridge of all.

Go through the gate on the left-hand side of the road (with your back
towards Kemble). Walk as near to the riverside as possible for a while
until the path — which is probably not very plain on the ground — runs
over the field towards a gap, blocked by a 12 foot length of fence, in
the hedge. On reaching the gap, turn right along a grassy track
with the hedge on your left. The track goes through a gate by a
footpath sign. Over to your right you will see a wind pump. Below
it is Lyd Well, possibly of Roman origin, a spring which at certain
times of the year produces the first Thames water.

Continue ahead, a hedge on the left, and notice away to the right a
slight dip in the ground which marks the line of the Thames.

Opposite a rather nice house of Cotswold stone the path bears right
and crosses the bed of the Thames at a point where some stones lying
around seem possibly to be the remains of an old bridge. The path
now runs towards a stone stile which leads into a road, the A429, the

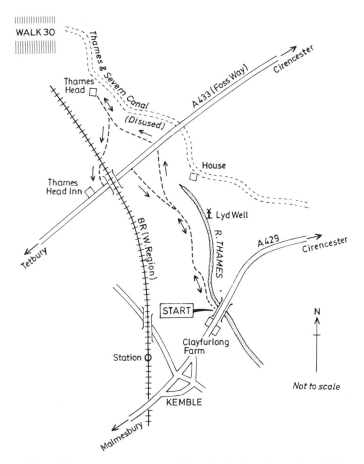

WALK 30

Thames & Severn Canal

Thames Head

(Disused)

A433 (Foss Way)

Cirencester

House

Thames Head Inn

Lyd Well

R. THAMES

A429 Cirencester

Tetbury

BR (W. Region)

START

Clayfurlong Farm

Station

N

Not to scale

KEMBLE

Malmesbury

Roman Foss Way. An extremely lofty (and therefore hopefully vandal-proof) footpath sign pinpoints the spot.

Having carefully crossed the road, which has become somewhat busier since the legions left, we see, lying back from it, an iron field gate giving access to a broad track ahead. This, in turn, leads to another iron gate opening into Trewbury Mead, a field enclosed by a beautiful dry stone wall. A track goes before us across the Mead towards a stone block — you can probably see it in the distance — surrounded by trees. You will find inscribed upon it: 'The Conservators of the River Thames 1857 - 1974. This stone was placed here to mark the source of the River Thames'. Formerly, there stood here a splendid statue of the bearded figure of Father Thames, but this has been prudently moved to a safer home beside St John's Lock at Lechlade, where you may have seen it on Walk 27.

A few loose stones lie around, indicating the spring where, occasionally, a little water rises. At one time there was a large well here, with water sufficient for the needs of the Roman garrison camped on the nearby mound called Trewbury Castle. It has been alleged that the construction at the end of the eighteenth century of the Thames and Severn Canal, now derelict, which lies a few yards above where we stand, probably had something to do with the present paucity of water, since it was a canal which depended upon pumping for its water supply and it was near here that water was pumped directly to the summit level from underground springs. But a water shortage was recorded earlier than that.

The geography of this area is such that I found it impossible to plan a proper circular walk to include the source of the Thames, though clearly such an important feature could not be omitted from this book. There is a route back, however, that is partly different. It has the advantage of passing close to a pub and the disadvantage of including a short stretch of busy road. So you can either retrace your steps to the car via the original route (the scenery always looks different going the other way) or try the alternative return route.

We start back in the direction in which we came, towards the iron gate in the dry stone wall, but divert towards a small wooden gate in the corner of the Mead to the right of the iron gate. Through this, a grassy path climbs slightly and comes to a stile giving access to a crossing of the railway. With the utmost care cross the railway lines. On the other side, climb a stile and, with the railway on your left, make your way along a broad track which widens out with many kinds of wild flowers in profusion all around. This was once a railway goods yard.

We leave it by a kissing gate and come out onto the Foss Way, or A429. Just to the right is the Thames Head Inn. Our direction, however, is to the left under the railway. Exercise extreme care here for the road is busy and the bridge narrow. A few yards beyond it, just after passing a road sign which says (as you will see when you have passed it) 'Oncoming Vehicles in Middle of Road', go through an iron gate on the right.

Pass down the field to a gate in the hedge on your left. Through this, the path runs rightwards. It soon merges with the route we took in the outward direction and we retrace our steps to the bridge and the car.

Thank you for joining me on these walks. I hope you have enjoyed discovering, as I have, how lovely is the Valley of England's greatest river.